CONTENTS

DEDICATION

To our families,
living and living still;

To our friends,
especially our closest;

To our counselees
who came out of need but remained by choice.

PREFACE

A word of explanation is necessary. Although two of us wrote this book, we chose to use the first person singular. This choice, we hope, adds to the flow of the stories we tell; it also reflects the result of many long hours of collaboration. We both contributed insights, haggled over differences, and revised our opinions as a result of working together. After refashioning several drafts (and throwing many of them away) and after resolving countless disagreements, we found that—without planning to do so—we were speaking with a single voice.

A word of assurance is called for. Throughout this book we tell stories about various people who struggled with the pain of loneliness and who had the courage to risk loving. Anyone who knows us knows that we're sticklers for confidentiality. We've gone to painstaking lengths to insure that no one's integrity is in anyway compromised.

A word of thanks is appropriate. Our families and friends taught us about love and they continue to do so. But the people we've seen in counseling have been our instructors as well. Their courage and at times unsettling honesty have prodded us to refine our thoughts, and their trust has made us willing to risk putting them in print. The contributions they've made to this book are clearly significant. The contributions they've made to our lives are far more priceless.

Everyone is Lonely

*I*n his mid-thirties, Brad Henderson was an administrator in a local hospital. He had called in sick on a number of occasions, due to migraine headaches, and when he spoke with a nurse practitioner at the personnel health clinic she referred him to me. Married for twelve years and father of two children, Brad struck me as a man accustomed to relating easily with people. During our first meeting, however, he seemed ill-at-ease. He was tense and he avoided talking about himself. He strayed off into detailed accounts of his job and seldom looked directly at me. When I asked about his reasons for coming to see me, he mentioned headaches and trouble sleeping. His wife complained that he had grown impatient with the children; he said that she was right and admitted that he was equally abrupt with people at work. He felt unappreciated by his boss, and he resented the man for not having supported his application for a promotion. Toward the end of the session, Brad admitted that he had begun having a few drinks before going to bed in order to help him fall asleep.

Brad's story came out in bits and pieces. He was anxious about so many things that at first he didn't know where to begin or what to say. His concerns about work seemed most important to him but they were intertwined with problems at home. Finally he stopped trying to sort things out and just let things tumble out in whatever way they did.

In my years as a counselor, I've learned it helps if people simply begin by talking about their problems and especially about what is causing them the most difficulty right now. Overwhelmed by pain and uncertain about its cause, they wonder—without explicitly asking the question—if I will understand. As I listen, ask questions, and show interest in what they say, they sense that I do appreciate what is happening to them and do care about the pain that they are experiencing.

Leaving my office at the end of the first session, Brad shook my hand and said, "Thanks for listening. I'm not sure what's going to come of all of this, but it sure feels good just to get it all out."

Brad's story reminded me of so many stories I've heard. The problems that bring people into my life initially seem so similar. In one form or another they all revolve around issues of identity or self-image and are concerned about one or another significant relationship. More often than not, a change or transition has deepened the pain to a point where the person involved is willing to risk coming to someone like me.

During his first few sessions, Brad talked about the conflicts he had with his boss and about the difficulties he faced as a supervisor and as a parent. Initially he spoke about things as if they were unrelated. He knew he had problems, but he failed to see any connections. As he continued to speak, however, he noticed patterns in his relationships, common ways he had of interacting with people. He explored changes he could make and he noticed that things got better. As he became more comfortable with me and as his problems grew less pressing, he started making use of our time together differently. He talked less about the immediacy of his problems and more about his past.

This is a common pattern. The longer people are with me, the more they want me to understand them, not just their problems. So they tell me about their lives, the sacred stories of their childhood, and all the while they're testing me at a deeper and deeper level to see if I can still understand them. They do so with trepidation and with hope, wondering if I will cherish what they share with me.

People's problems all look alike, that is, until I have listened carefully enough to draw close to them. The closer

I draw, the more I realize the uniqueness of each person and each problem. It's like fingerprints. At first glance, they too look alike, a mass of curves and whorls. But we know that no two prints are ever the same. Infinite variations make each print singular. So it is with people and their problems. At the outset, they look so similar. But with time and the opportunities a good relationship offers, significant differences slowly emerge. Because of these differences, no two people experience an event—even the same event—in exactly the same way. As a counselor, I listen to people enough so that I begin to hear their stories less from the outside in and more from the inside out.

Gradually, as I continue to listen to people's stories, it seems as if the stories fade in importance, their details become less significant. I never stop listening to the stories or paying attention to the details, but I find myself less caught up in the accounts and more involved with the person. Once I enter deeply enough into people's lives, I notice a whole new phenomenon. I realize that what makes us human is strikingly the same, not similar but shared. Again, it's like fingerprints. Experts tell us not only of their uniqueness and infinite variety but also of the basic underlying patterns shared by all.

The purpose of this book is to examine one of those shared patterns. It isn't the only pattern in our lives, although it is a pattern that is in each of us. It isn't experienced by everyone in the same way, although it is always a point of stress. It is the pattern of loneliness.

After several months of seeing me, Brad talked about his childhood memories. He was the younger son of a minister. As his father received calls from progressively larger churches, Brad and his family moved from one place to another. He was identified as the minister's son, and he hated the feeling that people expected him to behave. By nature, however, he was easy-going and he got along well with others. Afraid of moving and of losing whatever friends he made,

Brad found it difficult to attach himself too closely to any one person. He always wanted and never had a best friend.

When his father came home at the end of the day, tired from listening to other people's problems, he retreated to his study and closed the door. "I knew my father loved me," Brad said, "but I can't say that I actually knew him or that he knew me, for that matter." His mother, a quiet woman who rarely expressed her feelings, was a peace-maker. She refused to let Brad and his brother, Harold, fight or talk about their problems in front of others. Her refrain was, "Never air your dirty laundry in public." While his brother was less successful in academic work, he was more popular and he played on the football team. Brad liked baseball but never made the team. They were friendly rivals, but not close. Harold enjoyed being a minister's son and later became a minister himself, while Brad felt more and more at odds with the church and eventually stopped attending services. His parents did not understand his decision and felt that it was a personal slight.

People tell stories of their childhood or of the more recent past in such different ways. Some remember details vividly even years after the event. Some speak vaguely, recalling only a few incidents. Many of the stories describe a particular face. A father separated by divorce. A grandmother who died. A teenage friend who committed suicide. Some tell stories which evoke memories of failure and inadequacy, leaving remnants of guilt. They have to do with sex, school, work, or the end of a friendship. Strangely enough, some people tell stories of what seems like success, but their stories leave them feeling as if they never fit in. All these stories tell of loss and isolation and separation. All these stories tell of loneliness.

Brad called me one day, asking if he could come in earlier than his regularly scheduled appointment. He sounded anxious, so I arranged to see him the next morning. When he arrived at my office, he was distraught. After a few minutes of silence, he told me he had been thinking about our last few sessions. Reviewing his life more carefully than he had ever done before made him realize how isolated he had been from his family and friends. Then he paused and put his head down and began quietly to cry. He took a deep breath, and, still shaking, he looked at me with pained eyes and said, "You know, I realize now that I've never felt close to anyone. I've never felt that anyone has ever understood me, accepted me for who I am. Certainly not my family. And perhaps not even my wife. To tell you the truth, I can't even tell you I feel that close to my own kids."

As I listen to people, I recognize the loneliness that threads through their stories, but I hesitate to identify it for them. Loneliness is such an isolating experience that even to admit to being lonely unravels new strands of pain. At first people shy away from facing the experience and refuse to name it for what it is. People like Brad have shown me how painful acknowledging loneliness can be and how much courage it takes to lay hold of it, to say, "I'm lonely." We hate to admit that we are lonely to ourselves much less to others, but by refusing to do so we only make ourselves even more isolated.

Since loneliness runs through so many people's lives, I've tried to learn as much as I can about it not only from those I counsel but also from those who have written about it. Some people make distinctions between loneliness and aloneness, between loneliness and solitude. Others believe that loneliness can be a rich ground for self-awareness and growth. Without discounting their insights, I hear a stronger theme playing in the background of the stories told by lonely people: loneliness is painful and the source of great suffering.

Loneliness is painful and the source of great suffering. Now, undoubtedly good can come from pain and suffering. It's a common experience, one I've witnessed time and again, that people can endure unimaginable hurt and even agony and become stronger and more peaceful as a consequence. It's also undeniable that many people are simply crushed by suffering. But even if pain provides the opportunity for good to emerge, I refuse to call pain good. In the same way, I refuse to call loneliness good. Loneliness hurts. It is always painful. It is not good.

Many psychologists say that loneliness lies at the heart of mental illness; neuroses and psychoses are, in fact, unhealthy ways of avoiding the pain of its isolation. But the pain that sometimes pushes people into disabling mental illness can also prod them into love.

Loving and being loved eases the pain of loneliness but, strangely, it also intensifies it. The more deeply we enter into love, the more aware we become of our still unfulfilled longing—a longing which seems incapable of being fulfilled. To love is to be partially satisfied and partially hungry. If we had no hope of being loved, no hope of easing the pain, then we could give up. We could resign ourselves to being lonely. If, on the other hand, we ever completely experienced love—through and through and without end— we could rest secure. The human dilemma is to be caught between satisfaction and desire, fulfillment and longing. Religious people call this yearning an unnamed search for God. They claim that the God who placed this forever deepening hunger in the human heart is the only one who can satisfy it. Another name for this yearning is loneliness.

If those who love and are loved still feel lonely, how much lonelier are those who have never felt loved at all. Yet it's true: many people feel as though no one has ever loved them, not their parents, not their families, not people they call friends, not even their spouses.

Even more people suffer from having loved and lost. The most obvious losses come too quickly to mind, the deaths of parents, the loss of a spouse through death or divorce. The pain of former losses presses upon us so painfully that we rarely reflect on how many of them we have suffered. But if we pause for a moment, we can remember friends who left us abruptly through misunderstanding or betrayal, friends who drifted apart with time and distance, friends who grew cold for seemingly no reason at all. We can also recall those special people who died—a grandparent, a favorite teacher, a beloved neighbor. All the losses of the past add to our loneliness, and their pain weighs us down and makes us afraid of ever taking the risk of loving again. Fear and the reluctance to risk, understandable as they are, only contribute to our loneliness.

For most of us, loneliness is a combination of all these experiences. We know the feeling of loving and being loved and still wanting more. We fear we have never really been understood or loved at all. We carry the memories of being loved and of losing that love. At times our loneliness fades in intensity, and we bear it with relative ease. Life makes sense, and our work and relationships satisfy us. At other times we're so alone and in pain that we can't go on. Our lives come crashing down around us. Tensions in relationships, problems at work, added stress, major changes in our lives undermine our self-confidence and make us vulnerable. At these moments we tend to react in extremes. Some people see themselves as victims, powerless to do anything about the pain they feel, and depression overwhelms them. Others lunge desperately into new relationships, becoming easily infatuated and making some people more important than they are. They try to avoid their pain by escaping into work, sex, alcohol or drugs. Or they follow the latest guru who promises a quick and easy method of finding fulfillment and happiness.

During our last session, Brad and I reviewed the previous year and a half of our relationship. At first one crisis after another had made him feel lost and depressed. Sleeplessness, drinking, and worries about his job and marriage had made him face his problems. He wanted to do something about whatever was causing his pain. Throughout those early sessions he talked about his problems as though they were things to be solved. He used me as a professional, a resource to help him achieve what he wanted. Gradually as he gained greater control over his life, he began looking at me more directly and wanting me to know him as a person, not just as a problem. He wanted to know me, too, and began asking my opinion and wondering how I felt about him. He related to me less as just a professional and more as a person he valued.

It was then that Brad admitted the loneliness he felt and began to share with me the pain of his isolation. Paradoxically, he was doing at that very moment what he lamented he had never been able to do: he was caring about another person and allowing that other person to care about him. This very fact—when I pointed it out to him—gave him hope: a crisis became a new beginning.

Looking at how our relationship had developed and recognizing what he had accomplished, Brad slowly rebuilt his self-confidence. He began relating to other people in the same way. He felt closer to his wife and children. "My wife says it's as though I've fallen in love with her again," he reported, "but I'd say it's more that I've learned how to love her for the first time." He made friends with some of the people at work, and he noted how much more relaxed he felt around his boss.

"I've really come to care about you," Brad said, as he stood to leave. "I may not see you again, at least not on a regular basis, but I'm not afraid of losing you. I'm going to take you with me wherever I go."

It is difficult to move from loneliness into love.

People like Brad have taught me there is no easy path to follow, but they have also convinced me there is a way out of separation and loneliness. There is no clearly marked road map. There is no way leading us easily out of loneliness or delivering us all at once and with little effort to the place we seek. Although there will undoubtedly be companions along the route, the journey is one we must make ourselves.

And while no one can make it for us, we can't make it on our own. The journey itself and the companions we choose, the sharing of struggles and pain along the way, are the first steps toward love.

That's precisely what I offer in this book: some insights, some guidelines, some wisdom others have taught me, some hope gained from my own searching. I hope my reflections can help you move out of loneliness into love.

We
make
Ourselves
Lonely

We make ourselves lonely.

It sounds silly, if not unkind, to suggest that we are responsible for our loneliness. Clearly, no one wants to be lonely: we know only too well the pain of isolation. True, there are times when we seek solitude, needing to get away from everyone else and be by ourselves for a while. And at times we find ourselves separated from the people we love through no choice of our own. On other occasions we withdraw, backing away from people more or less consciously, to protect ourselves from the possibility of being rejected as we have been in the past. Still, we hate being lonely, and we would do anything at all to love and be loved.

But it's true that we make ourselves lonely.

Allison was forty-nine years old when she first came to see me. Instead of talking about recent events or why she needed help, she told me about her childhood and especially about her father. He was warm and affectionate, unlike her mother. Although Allison was often hurt by the things her mother said, she refused to cry in front of her, afraid she would be ridiculed. Her father held her whenever she was sad and rocked her gently, calling her "my little princess." Allison's parents fought constantly, and often when she was in bed at night she would hear them yelling at each other. She knew that they were talking about her and that her father always took her side.

He called himself a "social drinker," but as the tension at home continued to build he drank more and more. And his drinking added to the stress. Allison and her father grew closer as her parents drifted apart. On those nights when their fights were particularly bitter, he left his wife and came to sleep with Allison. Although she felt sorry for him and wished that her mother would stop being so unkind, she enjoyed having her father with her. He held her close and told her how much she meant to him. With time, as his trips to her bedroom grew more regular, he became sexually involved with her. She was eleven years old, and she was frightened and confused.

We've all been wounded by the people who love us. Allison isn't the only one who has scars to show and stories of neglect and abuse to tell. No one is perfect, and no one loves perfectly. When others love us, they do so imperfectly. Sometimes, in trying to love us, they harm us. All of us have been battered in one way or another, although we often imagine that we're the only ones who have ever suffered and that no one else can possibly understand what we've endured. At other times we think that our pain is nothing compared to what other people have gone through. But it makes no sense to compare our suffering with the pain of others or to wonder whether we have more or less reason to hurt than they do. We all ache, and the question is not "How great is my pain?" nor "Do I have a right to hurt?" The real question is "What do I do with my hurt, with the memories and the scars I bear?"

When Allison left home to go to college, she met a man who was attracted to her. He was in his mid-thirties, a graduate teaching assistant in one of her classes. He said he loved her and wanted to take care of her. Although she didn't love him, she liked the way he watched out for her. He made her feel secure. When he proposed to her, she accepted. Two months before their wedding date, they were in an accident. He was killed, and her face was badly scarred.

She never married. "Who would have me?" she asked. "I was never much to look at in the first place, and now look at me."

Every time we talk about ourselves, either to ourselves or to others, we tell stories of what has happened to us and of what we have done in the past. But we have to be careful about how we tell our stories. Like water flowing over rock, our stories slowly mold how we see ourselves. As we report, "These are the events of my life," we're actually saying, "This is who I am and why I do what I do." We all have stories which are particularly important to us, and the more we repeat them the more they shape the contours of our self-understanding. The events themselves—as critical as they may be—have less power to form us than the way we recall and talk about them.

As Allison recounted her past, first to herself and later to me, she told of how love always brought pain and loss and, in doing so, she defined how she saw herself. Her stories of neglect, abuse, and loss created a clear image in her own mind of herself: she was, in her words, "damaged goods," incapable of loving or being loved.

In a way, there is no past but the way we remember it, the way we recall it, the way we talk about it. Our stories of the past fashion our vision of the present, how we see ourselves and others and what we expect of life and the world. Stories have power, and we have to be careful how we tell them or else they will lock us into present self-identities which are as unchangeable as the past itself. When we let the past determine how we see ourselves in the present, we limit what we can do and how we can relate here and now. When we say, "I am what I am because of the way people loved me or failed to love me or because of the things that have happened to me," we usually mean, "I am what happened to me in the past and I can't do anything about it." At first we let the past shape our identities and mind-sets and in the end we use the past as an excuse, a reason why we can't be or do anything differently.

We are not totally free of the past. What has happened to us leaves its mark on our self-perceptions, on our feelings, and on our ability to respond to people and events. We are not able to create at any moment a new shape of ourselves as if out of thin air. Things from the past, things that we did not choose and over which we had no power—like our families, for example—will always play a part in making us who we are. But we have the power in the present to decide how those things are going to affect us and how much influence they will have in our lives. And that power comes from the way we tell our stories.

As Allison described her pain so vividly, I understood why she thought of herself as pathetic and helpless. I saw her misfortune through her own eyes and I felt her grief and anger, and I became helpless, just like her. At first she appreciated my sympathy, my ability to identify with her pain. She had never talked to people about her family or about her college years because she feared that they would laugh at her or, worse yet, blame her. My acceptance gave her reason to believe that she wasn't strange, and for a while she was relieved. But then, realizing that I was as confused as she was and as unable to do anything to change her life, she became distraught. I had confirmed in her own mind that she was indeed helpless. "What hope is there for me," she asked in tears, "if even you can't see any way out of my misery?"

Our stories shape how we see ourselves: they also shape how others see us. They hear the same message we tell ourselves: "This is who I am; this is what the past has made me." When we tell others about our lives, recalling our past hurts and losses, we let them know us as we know ourselves, and they see us as we see ourselves. That's both a blessing and a curse. It's reassuring to realize that others understand us even when we can't make much sense out of our own lives. Often it's comforting just to hear someone say, "I know how you're feeling." On the other hand, when people get so close to us that they identify with our problems and feelings, they lose perspective and we lose the chance to see ourselves differently. We've already determined in our own minds who we are and what we can expect of the world by the way we tell and retell our stories. As we do so, we are also presenting the same image to others, and when they believe our stories and accept our conclusions they reinforce our way of seeing ourselves.

Allison portrayed herself as life's helpless victim, and when I listened to her story and felt her pain I unconsciously confirmed her self-image.

We need people to listen to us with care, people who will love us enough to hear our stories both with acceptance and with a certain amount of distance. Their understanding and sympathy give us the support we need to take new risks; after all, it's risky to let others catch a glimpse of what goes into making us who we are. But we also need the insight and perspective which they can provide only if they maintain a little distance. It can be unsettling but helpful when someone says, "You know, I can understand why you see things the way you do, but I'm not sure that's the only way to look at it. Let me tell you how I see it."

Allison convinced herself that she was hopeless, and then she convinced me. In turn, my inability to see any alternatives, my hopelessness, reinforced her own self-appraisal. What hope was there for her, if even I—the professional, the expert—got caught in her hopelessness?

When Allison asked "What hope is there for me if even you can't see any way out of my misery?" she jolted me into realizing that I had become caught up in her story. I had fallen into the same trap she was in: the belief that her past, absolutely and for all time, held her prisoner. I felt powerless, and I got a clue into her powerlessness. I had simply followed the same path she had walked and I arrived at the same destination: the inability to change and the inevitability of failure. To be of any help, I had to do what she was incapable of doing. I had to focus on the present. I had to break the bonds of the past by refusing to make it all-powerful.

When I stopped recalling the sad and sometimes sick-ening events of her past and instead looked at her, I saw a forty-nine year old who was making herself miserable. There was no denying that others had caused her pain in the past, but it was equally clear that she was the one in the present who was taking advantage of herself. Without intending to do so and not even knowing what she was doing, she was using the past and its pain to keep herself immobilized.

I asked, "Allison, can you tell me what's happening right here, between the two of us, right this minute?"

Surprised by the question, she responded immediately, "I don't know."

"I think you do."

"I don't know what you mean."

"It just happened again," I said. "You're doing with me right now what you've been doing with your whole life. You didn't search for an answer to my question. You didn't struggle to understand what was going on. You gave up. You said you didn't know."

Allison shook off my persistent questions. Her voice grew weak and whiny, and her eyes got watery as if she were going to cry. She started to sound and to look like a victim.

I refused to back down. "I need to know what's going on right now. I need to hear it from you, and until you can tell me I don't see how we can go on."

She began to pout, but I continued to push her. She became frustrated, silent, and then angry. Finally, she blurted out, "I don't have to take this from you, you know."

She was right, of course. She didn't have to put up with my questions or my tone of voice. That was precisely the point: she had more freedom than she thought she had and more ability to respond to people's actions than she was willing to claim. Finding herself in a situation which par-alleled so many of the other painful events of her life—of being hurt by someone who loved her—she had to decide what to do. The simplest thing would be to repeat her old patterns, to walk away from me. She could tell herself and others, if they asked, that I was a callous and insensitive man who had initially shown her care but had eventually turned on her, just like the others in her life. She could blame me as she had blamed all the other people who had hurt her in the past. She could cry and say to herself, "Poor me," and she could probably get others to agree with her and say, "Poor Allison." In that case, she would have one more story to tell, one more confirmation that she was indeed a victim of other people's lack of care, one more justification for not doing anything to change her life.

Then again, she could change.

I presented her with a situation which paralleled—in a way—other painful ones from her past. She felt caught in a relationship like so many former ones, helpless and afraid. But this time things were different. I appreciated what she was feeling and thinking, but I refused to play the role she had assigned me. She felt like a victim, but I would not allow her to portray me as the victimizer.

It was her choice.

She didn't get up and walk away. Instead, she said, "I know you're doing this for my good, but it's very hard."

"You're right. I know it's hard for you. But tell me, what just happened here between you and me?"

"What do you mean?"

I refused to answer.

After a pause, she replied, "Well, I lost my temper and yelled at you."

"I'll tell you something. You sound a lot more adult to me when you're yelling than when you're whining."

"But I wasn't whining."

"That's what it sounded like to me. I think you've been whining most of your life. Sure, you've had more than your fair share of pain and hardship. But it seems to me that you've never stood up to it. You've let it run you over like a Mack truck. You've become your own worst enemy."

We all are our own worst enemies.

23

There's no denying that other people have hurt us. People we depended on, people who had a lot of influence in our lives, people like our parents, have at times been unkind and even cruel. It's easy to judge them and to put them down for their failures and inadequacies, but it doesn't get us anywhere. They're like us, caught in a cycle of being hurt by others who love poorly and in turn hurting others by loving poorly.

Allison was neglected by her mother and abused by her father, and she had reason to hurt. But what about them? What had happened to Allison's mother to make her cold and controlling? And what had happened to her father? There's no justifying what her parents did to her or what some people have done to us, but blaming them does no one any good. To blame people for the pain they have caused keeps us from taking responsibility for our own lives. People have hurt us and, no matter how understandable or reprehensible their actions, we hurt. But no matter how much others have hurt us in the past, we are the ones who hurt ourselves in the present.

We hurt ourselves by telling the same old stories over and over again, by reliving the pain of the past, by giving up and handing our power over to people who may be long dead or far away. In all of this, we are very active, but in a strange way: we are actively choosing to be passive. We make it look as though the harm is done by other people or by our past and, in a way, of course, that's true. But the real truth of the matter is that we harm ourselves even more by giving up any hope of changing. Since people failed to love us in the past, we see ourselves as unlovable and we give up any hope of being loved.

Being lonely looks like something that is done to us, but in reality it is something we do to ourselves. We make ourselves powerless, we avoid taking risks or initiating new relationships, and in doing so we choose to be lonely.

Allison admitted that she didn't like how she sounded when she whined. It made her feel like a little girl. She examined the way she related to people and the things she did to keep them at a distance. After talking over several possibilities with me, she decided she wanted to get to know better a woman she worked with. The woman, Judy, was her age, and Allison had helped her learn the office routines and policies when she first started the job. Allison liked Judy and thought Judy might like her, but both women seemed too shy to talk about much other than work. Allison considered asking her out to lunch, but as we talked I could see her waver and back down. She knew she had to do something to break out of her pattern of avoidance, but when she thought about actually doing something specific, she froze. Step-by-step we talked about what she could do. How would she begin the conversation? What would she say? Where would they meet? We even acted out the situation so Allison could have a feel for what might happen. At the end of the session, she set off, feeling both determined and excited.

Allison dragged herself into our next meeting, discouraged. She had not talked to Judy. Instead she had decided to meet with her mother. "I thought," she said, "I might as well go all the way since I'm starting fresh. I've avoided my mother all my life. She's the one I should face." She set up a lunch date with her mother, and as usual her mother was late. When she did arrive, she dominated the conversation and never once asked Allison about herself. She was rude to the waiter, complained about the food, and criticized Allison's dress. Allison felt awkward and embarrassed, and never said a word of the speech she had prepared and memorized the night before. She felt like a failure. "What's the use?" she asked. "I'm no better off than I was before."

"It sounds as though you want me to pity you," I said. She glared at me.

"That's the last thing I'm going to do," I continued. "You set yourself up to fail."

She was livid. She called me heartless and cruel, said I didn't care about her, and told me she was tired of being made to feel stupid.

"Do you mean," I asked, "that you're tired of making yourself feel stupid?"

"What do you mean?"

"You think about it," I replied. "How was setting up this lunch with your mother any different from other ways you've set yourself up to fail and be rejected?"

Allison reflected for a while. "I guess I made myself a victim again, didn't I?"

At times when I'm working with someone like Allison, I propose a "let's pretend" game.

I ask them to pretend that the past was an accident. It was an unexpected and unfortunate event over which they had no control. Now, they know as well as I that it wasn't really an accident. They were graced with moments of love and many good things happened along with the pain. And they had more say in shaping their lives than they want to admit. Still, there are times when they feel like the victim of a past that was wildly out of control, disabled by a jolting and irreversible event or string of events.

I say, "Why don't you indulge your bleakest fantasies of the past? Imagine that every painful event and relationship was simply part of one colossal accident. You can't change it. There's nothing you can do to make the past any different than it is. What are you going to do now?"

Even if the worst about our past is true—even it is all a mishap—we still have choices to make in the present.

We can give up. We might feel paralyzed or blinded or scarred by our past—unable to trust ourselves or anyone else. We can throw up our arms in resignation, bemoan our fate, and complain that life isn't fair. Initially, that's what Allison did. She thought of herself as weak and defenseless, unable to love and be loved, capable only of feeling sorry for herself.

We can take on the impossible. If the past has made us reluctant to talk about our feelings, we can try to express all our emotions all the time. If the past has given us reason to be afraid of people we don't know, we can try to be the most out-going persons in the world. It's as though we've been flat on our backs in a hospital bed for six weeks and we decide on our first day up we have to run the Boston Marathon. Of course, we fail. Tackling the impossible is simply a disguised way of giving up, since it guarantees failure. That's what Allison did when she tried to confront her mother. She took on too much. She may have thought she was making a daring change. After all, wasn't facing her mother the opposite of avoiding her? Actually, though, she had merely discovered—unconsciously, perhaps—a new way of getting herself rejected. Taking on too much not only insures failure, it gives us an excuse not to try again. Allison's failure with her mother gave her a reason not to reach out even to the woman at work. "What's the use in trying?"

If we're tired of giving up—either directly or indirectly—there's something else we can do. Let me suggest what this is by using the example of physical therapy. The parallels between what happens in physical therapy and in counseling are striking.

Following an accident, physical therapy is slow and demanding work. Patients often feel desolated, despairing that they'll ever walk again. The therapist might begin by massaging muscles that have grown slack, loosening joints and getting the circulation going. Next, an exercise pool is used where water reduces the stress and where patients can move about more easily and with less threat of falling. Gradually, after their muscles have been strengthened they begin working in a specially designed room, supporting themselves with braces and hand rails. Only after hours, weeks, sometimes years of exercise and practice can they finally stand unaided. There are constant setbacks, and at each step of the way patients border on giving up, thinking they've progressed as far as they can.

The same is true whenever we take on new behavior. The past may be an accident, leaving us weak in some places and disabled completely in others, but we can still live as fully and as responsibly as possible. It takes a lot of work and even more time to make changes in our lives, especially changes which are as basic as the way we love. It takes a regimen that involves repeated failure, new attempts, and incremental improvements. We've learned to relate to people the way we do through a lifetime of encounters, and those years of learning can't be refashioned overnight. Instead, we have to exercise underdeveloped resources and train ourselves to compensate for disabilities.

That's what was happening with Allison. At first, she began testing out new ways of relating with me. It was painful for her and she kept thinking that I was pushing her too hard, but eventually she felt more confident, ready to try engaging others. After the disaster with her mother, she decided to set up a lunch date with the woman at work, a small but important step.

This sort of change is painful, and the results—when they come—are often small and unremarkable. We can strengthen a flagging self-image, for example, by affirming ourselves for little accomplishments and by patting ourselves on the back each time we succeed at something new. It's the little things we do over and over again that make a difference. We can expect setbacks. We can count on hurting and wanting to give up. But we can work all the harder to develop the ability to love and be loved.

After three years, Allison decided she no longer needed to see me. "I like the sound of that," she said. "I don't need you. I appreciate all you've done for me and you'll always be special. I couldn't have done the things I've done without you. But I don't need you. Not the way I used to. Not as though I'm some helpless little girl who can't do anything for herself."

Allison didn't introduce any startling changes into her life, but she did come to feel better about herself and to trust other people. She made friends at work, and she became involved with a church group that visited a nursing home.

She talked about a man she had met. "He's a bit younger than I am," she said almost apologetically but, catching the whine in her voice, she immediately smiled and added, "but at least he doesn't remind me of my father."

We make ourselves lonely. We do so by the way we remember the past, by the way we tell stories of what has happened to us, by the way we give up any hope of changing our lives. It sounds depressing to think that we are the ones responsible for our own loneliness. How could we cause ourselves so much pain? And yet admitting our part in making ourselves lonely gives us a lot of power. If we make ourselves lonely, we can also make ourselves loving. If we chose to isolate ourselves, we can also choose to love.

Why choose Loneliness?

*S*o why do we do it?

Why, if loneliness hurts, do we choose to be lonely? It is, following the two previous chapters, logical to ask that question, although it isn't at all a logical question. Or, at least, it isn't a question that allows for a logical answer.

In theory no one would deny that loneliness hurts, but in practice we've mastered countless ways of discounting its pain—some of them conscious, most of them unconscious. For a while, we can forget it, block it out, dull it with alcohol or drugs, or hide from it by plunging into work and never-ending activities. We don't want to admit that we're lonely—it makes us feel as though we're failures, as though there's something wrong with us—but even more we hate acknowledging how deeply we hurt. In a society that values strength and independence, especially in men, pain embarrasses us. But even when we successfully deny our loneliness and pain, there's a part of us that knows, that won't be silenced, that quietly admits, "This loneliness I feel—sometimes more, sometimes less—is always painful."

There isn't any part of us, not the tiniest bit, willing to admit that we choose to be lonely. Everything in us rises up in protest, "I didn't do it. It's not my fault." We exhaust ourselves looking for love. We can laugh or cry at some of what we've done to make love last, but it's hard not to cry when we realize that the very ways we've tried to escape loneliness have only led us more surely into its cell. One man I know used to go to singles' bars five nights a week. He drank and danced, shouted inane comments into women's ears even though he knew they couldn't hear him over the music. But the end of the night was always the same: he worried about finding someone to accompany him home for the night. At first he told me it was his empty house—he was recently divorced—that made him so lonely. When I let him know I could understand the intensity of his loneliness, an intensity that drove him out of his home and into the singles' bars, he felt less need to defend his behavior. He admitted that his nightly jaunts only left him feeling lonelier than ever. "Who am I kidding?" he asked. "After a while, it was just plain hard work. There wasn't any love involved. To be honest, there was precious little pleasure." What seems at first a choice to love is often a choice that makes us lonely.

If we admit—even grudgingly—that being lonely is painful and—even more reluctantly—that we choose it nevertheless, is there any way to make sense of what we do? The question—"Why, if loneliness hurts, do we choose to be lonely?"—isn't a logical question. And it doesn't allow for a logical answer because it's shot through with apprehensions and assumptions that aren't at all logical.

We choose to be lonely even though it hurts because we're afraid of something that hurts even more: rejection. We know the pain of loneliness, but we fear even more the pain of being rejected by someone else. It's not as though we consciously choose loneliness instead of rejection; the alternatives rarely stand out so clearly. Rather, we instinctively protect ourselves from the awful possibility of being rejected, and we do so in ways that leave us lonely. We react to people without much thought or self-awareness. We avoid certain subjects. We let others see the parts of ourselves we value and steer them clear of the hurting or fearful parts. We love cautiously and partially, and we allow others to love us in the same way. And we do so over and over again until at last our ways of loving and being loved become so ingrained in us that we can't imagine any other possibility— any other possibility, that is, besides being rejected.

We make ourselves lonely because we doubt we can really be loved. We expect to be rejected.

At heart we believe, "If you knew me, you wouldn't love me." We're convinced there's something about us that is sick or repulsive or wrong, and as soon as others see what it is they'll run away from us, screaming in fright. It's as though each of us has a little box inside us, and we stuff it full of all the awful things we've done or felt or thought. Things other people have done to us or said about us get stashed in there, too. Anger, pettiness, spite, sexual urges, and whatever else makes us feel ugly and bad get crammed inside. At times we're terrified that the box will explode and the mess will splatter all over everyone, but most of all we're afraid that the people we care about will get too close and ask to see what's inside.

We love being loved—to a point.

When people love us, they want to know more and more about us. They want to see what's inside us. What do we think about and value? What's most important to us? Whom do we care about and how much do we care? At first we're delighted that people find us interesting, complimented by their questions and willingness to listen. But sooner or later our delight turns to apprehension. We begin to worry. We think we can only be loved as long as people don't know us too well. We fear they'll finally stumble upon the dark secret we've been hiding, and when they do they'll turn away.

"You'll probably think I'm strange," Karl explained when I asked why he wanted to talk to me, "but I'm here because I'm twenty-nine years old and I've fallen in love for the first time. She's the best thing that's ever happened to me. I've told her things about myself I've never told anyone else, and she makes me feel special."

"So tell me again why you're concerned."

"I don't want to lose her. I know she loves me and she says she'll never leave me and I want to believe her. But there's stuff I've done I just can't let her know about, stuff I'm not real proud of. She'd leave me if she knew, I know she would. And I can't say I'd blame her. But I don't want to lose her."

Since we're convinced people will leave us once they see what's inside, our only hope is to keep them at just the proper distance: close enough to love us but far away enough not to know us. And if they get too close, we laugh and change the subject, become passive or speak in generalities—do anything to lead them away from that dread secret box. A woman told me about the time her fiancé had invited her to a picnic and a bicycle ride in the country. She turned him down, saying that bikes were for kids, and anyway it would mess up her hair. The truth of the matter was that as a child she had been teaching her younger brother to ride a bicycle, and when she wasn't watching he swerved into the street and was hit by a car. He was paralyzed by the accident, and in a way so was she. Thirteen years later, her insides were as disabled as her brother's legs. In her head she knew she ought to be able to tell her friend what had happened, but in her heart she was afraid of taking the risk. She kept him away from her guilt. He didn't know her pain; he only felt the distance. He felt rejected and eventually he stopped seeing her.

How can we tell those who love us and ask what's bothering us, "I'm afraid you'll see the real me, all the mess I've stored away, and you'll stop loving me"?

Sometimes we fear rejection so much that we defend ourselves against it by rejecting first. We keep others at a distance—we reject them—thinking it's better to walk away from them than to allow them to put us down.

Sometimes, depending on how much we're willing to risk, we open the box a crack and allow the briefest glimpse of what's inside. Since we've been holding the lid down for such a long time, there are all sorts of experiences and feelings huddled together in the dark. Now, at the first sign of light, they come stampeding out, not single-file, but in droves. If, for example, we've compacted all our anger, holding it in, it's likely to leap out roaring, vicious, and eager to pounce on the nearest victim. After we've done or said something that hurts others, we realize why we kept the lid on our anger in the first place; we make up our minds never to express it again and so it continues, reinforced and stronger than ever.

Once I asked a friend why he disliked holidays, and he set off on a rampage about family gatherings and people drinking too much and everyone expecting him to be perfect and why couldn't they understand he didn't want to be like them anyway. Finally, he ran out of breath, looked at me sheepishly, and added, "I guess you got more than you bargained for."

When people catch sight of what we've been holding in, they do occasionally react as we expect them to: they reject us. Their rejection may have nothing—or almost nothing—to do with us. Our insecurity blinds us to other people's insecurities, and we never stop to think that they're harboring as many hurts and fears as we are. One woman, Christine, told me how ashamed she was for deserting her best friend when she needed her most. Her friend had been raped. "I did what I could do for her, you know," she said. "I held her and let her cry. I stayed with her and let her talk. But all the time, I could feel myself shriveling up. I can't stand being with her now, and she knows it." What her friend doesn't know is what Christine couldn't bring herself to talk about: that she had been raped when she was fifteen. All her friend knows is that she has been rejected. When someone rejects us we may not know why, but we assume it's our fault. After all, we expect to be rejected.

Sometimes people reject us and it is our fault, or, at least, it's more of our doing than we're aware of or would like to admit. Their closeness makes us nervous: if they come near enough to see us as we are, they'll surely leave us. And so—to keep their love—we need them to back off; we push them away in the hope of holding onto them. It's a muddled message, of course, since we seem to be repelling the people we most want to keep. We say, in effect, "I care about you, but stay away." Unfortunately, all too often people hear the last words of the statement more clearly than the first and they leave us. They feel rejected by us; we feel rejected by them.

One member of a therapy group I led, a young man named Ted, was withdrawn and passive. He looked bored, although sometimes he seemed frightened. After a number of sessions the other participants tried to draw him out. They asked him to talk about himself, but he became even more remote. One told him, "Look, Ted, we've all taken risks. You've got to start sometime. That's why we're here. You can't just sit there and watch us make fools of ourselves. If you want to be part of the group, you're going to have to let us know you." Finally, he blurted out that he had joined the group to overcome his fear of people. His parents had abandoned him, and he had been moved from one foster home to another. "I hate my parents," he was nearly screaming, "I hate everyone, and I hate all of you, too." The vehemence in his voice silenced the group, and they became withdrawn.

Our efforts to keep people from getting too close often backfire and drive people away from us completely.

At the very moment Ted had opened the lid of his box to us for the first time, he got frightened and slammed it shut. In any place other than a therapy group, Ted's outburst would have left him isolated and feeling rejected. But a group allows people to learn new behavior, so I asked the other members what they were feeling and what they wanted to say to Ted. One woman spoke up: "Ted, I feel awful about what happened to you, but that's not to say I think you're awful. I'm scared of your anger. I'm also scared of your pain. My first impulse is to run away, but I don't want to do that." Others joined in. They told Ted that they felt closer to him because of what he had revealed about himself but that they also felt attacked, repelled not by *what* he had told them but by *how* he had told them. He cried. "This is the first place I've ever felt safe. I don't hate you. I'm scared. Whenever I opened my mouth before, I've always gotten hurt. I'm just scared."

We may never know why people reject us—it may be their fears or ours or a combination of both—but whatever the reason, whenever someone leaves us it confirms our fear that we can't be known and loved.

Once in a while, though, people surprise us. After making some self-revelation that shames us, we wince and inwardly steel ourselves against the inevitable blow, only to encounter a nonplussed gaze which seems to say, "What's so bad about that?" Dumbfounded, we ask, "Didn't you hear what I said? Don't you see what I'm really like? And if so, why aren't you headed for the door?"

At some level we all believe, "If you knew me, you wouldn't love me." Many of us might point to someone, perhaps a husband, wife, or friend, who does know us and love us. Still their love doesn't resolve the nagging doubt that we're basically unlovable. It isn't true that we cannot be known and loved, only that we *believe* we cannot be known and loved. The belief is present in all of us from the beginning, although it can be altered gradually and not without setbacks. Even when—especially when—we have been accepted and loved, we know how rare it is. At first we were cautious, we trusted in little ways, always testing the other person's acceptance of us, and we vacillated between delight and the dread that things would soon fall apart. We consider ourselves fortunate to have found or to have been found by one other person—maybe more than one— capable of loving us as we are. We expect love to be the exception, not the rule; we doubt it at first and many times along the way, and we rejoice when it proves true—all because our basic conviction is that we can't be known and loved.

It rarely fails. At some point in counseling, people come face to face with their self-doubt, the ingrained sense that they're no good and unworthy of being loved. And they ask, "Why?"

Jim majored in both pre-law and pre-medicine. He was rated first in his class at a prestigious university. He was handsome, athletic, and easy to talk to. He came to see me after a doctor had been unable to find a medical basis for his recurring headaches. "It doesn't take a genius to see what I'm doing," Jim told me one day not long after we had begun meeting. "Work, succeed, achieve—that's what I do to prove myself."

"Prove yourself?"

"Yeah. I used to think I had to prove myself to my father. He's a surgeon, and I've always respected him. He constantly pushed me to be the best I could be. You know, to succeed."

"You said, 'I used to think . . . .' "

"Well, lately I'm not so sure. Maybe I'm the one I have to convince. Dad's proud of me, I know that. He's the one who's been trying to get me to ease up on myself. But I can't stop pushing. I'm never satisfied. If I score 97 percent on a test, I'm disappointed. Why didn't I get a 100 percent? It doesn't matter that no one else scored higher. I should have been perfect."

"What's it like to be perfect?"

"I don't know. I never make it. No matter how well I do, I always feel as though something's missing."

"Like what?"

"Like, why can't I feel good about myself? You know, it's funny—but funny isn't the word. People tell me they envy me, that I'm lucky to be me, but I sure don't feel that way. I feel rotten. And I just wish I could feel okay about being myself."

Why is it so hard to feel good about ourselves? Why is it so easy to deny our worth and to doubt that anyone can really love us?

Sometimes answers leap to mind. There's a horde of them huddled in our secret box—mistakes we've made, injuries we've suffered, fantasies we've entertained—and all of them, singly or combined, tell us we're no good. Most of the time we aren't troubled by the box or its contents. It's as though we've stationed a guard on its lid to protect us from the mess inside. But every so often and without warning, one painful incident sneaks past the sentry and springs open the lid. Everything we fear and hate about ourselves charges out of the box and attacks our self-esteem, leaving us devastated.

Jim sat in my office one day, looking dejected. "My chem lab instructor hopped all over my case today," he said. "Told me I was doing the whole procedure wrong and called me incompetent. Said he expected better things of me." Normally Jim would have explained what had happened, acknowledged his mistakes, and corrected what he was doing. But this time he excused himself, went to his dorm room, and wept. "It was like every failure in my life hit me in the face," he told me later. "Breaking up with my first girl friend. The time I was caught cheating on a test. I even remembered my father scolding me for breaking his favorite golf club, and that was twelve years ago."

It's a common occurrence. One painful incident calls to mind several painful memories.

For the most part we know only too well why we feel the way we do about ourselves, but sometimes we simply can't understand why we feel as bad about ourselves as we do. It's not that we can't list the regrets, losses, and guilt that undermine our self-esteem. It's just that when we add up all the feelings and frightening memories, the total doesn't tally with the intensity of self-rejection. We can understand why we feel bad about ourselves but not why we feel *so* bad. We wonder if there's something more, something we're not aware of, to explain our feelings.

After numerous sessions, Jim reported feeling even worse than before. His headaches came more frequently, and he found it increasingly difficult to sleep through the night. "I know I've asked it before," he said, "but now I really want to know. Why do I feel so terrible? Sure, I've done some pretty stupid things, but nothing spectacularly bad. And while I'll be the first to admit I haven't had the happiest of lives, I really can't complain about anything in particular. I honestly can't think of anything I've done or that's been done to me that's all that bad. And yet I feel terrible about myself. I mean, terrible."

We're all capable of forgetting painful events, at least for a while. It's as though we put the feelings on hold, waiting for a time when we feel more able to cope with them. Sometimes it's a conscious decision: "I'll deal with that later." Sometimes we don't even know we're doing it. A woman, for example, reported how she had reacted when she and her son were in a car accident. It was a major pile-up, involving several vehicles, and a number of people were killed. She said she acted like a machine, feeling nothing at all while she moved her son to safety. When the ambulances arrived and he was taken care of, she began to weep. It was only then that she realized how much the scene had repulsed her and how frightened she had been and that she had broken her collarbone and ribs. There's nothing wrong with postponing feeling for a while. Under some conditions, it might be the healthiest thing we can do. But putting off pain or forgetting its source doesn't make it go away. Eventually we have to face it.

"I don't know," Jim said. "Maybe I'm repressing something. I don't remember anything all that bad about my childhood, but then I can't remember much of anything about it."

Jim started talking about his older brother who had died when he was four. He remembered his brother only indistinctly, more from stories others had told and from old photographs than from his personal memory. He couldn't recall anything about the death or the funeral except what his parents had told him. His brother was killed in a car accident. Over a long period of time Jim began to piece together his memory of the event, and as he did so he became anxious. Finally during one session he stared into the distance as though he were witnessing something and he suddenly turned pale.

"My brother and I were playing in the driveway," he said more to himself than to me. "John was on his tricycle— it was too little for him—and I was on a scooter. Dad came barreling out of the garage—he was probably rushing to the hospital—and backed the car over John." Jim had seen it all but he had never grieved for his brother. Now he sobbed.

We have, hidden in our secret boxes, countless reasons to feel bad about ourselves, to doubt that anyone can know us and still love us. At first we think our boxes are large but simple, like old trunks with one wide open compartment and perhaps a tray that lifts out. Once we open the lid— inadvertently, reluctantly, or consciously—we discover all sorts of fears and hurts, sometimes neatly sorted, frequently in disarray, but always in ample supply. But our boxes aren't nearly as simple as they first appear. Even after we've unpacked all they contain and examined every corner, we're left with the disquieting sense that there's something more still to be found. Our boxes are more like a magician's chest than an old trunk. They're constructed with drawers, hidden compartments, and false bottoms. Many of the reasons we feel the way we do about ourselves are stored in the main sections and open areas, but our most painful memories are often secreted away in less accessible sections, hidden in concealed compartments. We can remove everything from our boxes, turn them upside down and shake them, but we can never be sure they're really empty. We can never account for everything in us that makes us feel rejected, unwanted, abused. There are always more reasons to distrust ourselves and our ability to be loved than we can ever lay our hands on.

After Jim mourned the loss of his brother, he was no longer bothered by headaches or sleeplessness. He felt relaxed and was able to concentrate once more on his studies, but he wasn't satisfied. "I know you're probably getting tired of my asking this question," he said one session, "but I still can't understand why I don't feel better about myself. I don't feel rotten anymore, that's for sure. I don't even feel really bad. But I don't feel great, either. Every time I think I've dealt with what's bugging me, something else pops up to take its place. I wonder at times if I'm just looking for reasons to get down on myself."

Jim isn't the only one who constantly finds new reasons to question himself. If a hundred things happen to us in a day but one of them is painful or causes anxiety, we invariably remember that one thing at the end of the day. We can empty our boxes—more or less—and uncover as many of the hidden compartments as possible, accepting the pains and losses, the griefs and injuries of our lives. And yet the next time we look, our boxes still have things that disturb us.

My grandmother was a compulsive house cleaner. Untiring in her campaign against dirt, she considered dust a personal affront. In the corner of her living room she stationed a large arrangement of pampas grass, silvery plumes that looked like an overgrown feather duster. Each week she would take the arrangement outside and shake it vigorously, sending clouds of dust billowing into the air. One day I commented how strange it was that she, of all people, had something in her house that seemed to serve no other function than to attract dust, her avowed enemy. She laughed and said, "But, silly, that's exactly why I keep it. It just sits there in the corner and sort of reaches out and grabs hold of all the dust in the room. It's my dust collector. It is to dust what fly paper is to flies."

There's something about us that collects negativity, that

gathers all the free floating anxiety and rejection we encounter each day and holds onto it. Reasons for self-doubt, like dust particles, fill the air—we're limited and prone to failure and unfaithfulness and so are those we live and work with—and through the years enough reasons have settled on us to convince us that we can't count on love. Even if we were able to shake loose all the damaging memories and fears, before long and without our knowing how or when it happened we'd find ourselves covered once more. There are reasons from our past—long forgotten or more recently encountered—why we distrust love and I suspect there will always be new ones. But all the reasons—real or imagined, past, present or future—can't entirely explain why we feel unlovable. What is there about us that attracts negativity, that is to pain and rejection what pampas grass is to dust? Or, returning to an earlier image, why do we have secret boxes that are so well suited to holding and concealing whatever causes us to doubt ourselves?

From the beginning we tend toward self-doubt; we allow the hurtful experiences that bump against us to cling to us and cover over our feelings of self-worth. Even if, with time and hard work, we clear away the residue of our past pains and come to a more affirming self-image, we constantly have to resist new accumulations. From the beginning—that is, from birth—we tilt toward self-doubt.

Newborn babies are the symbols of innocence. They're a fresh start, a new beginning, unlimited potential. As adults we see ourselves as just the opposite. Choices we've made over the years and those made for us limit us and what we can do. There are talents we don't possess, qualities we haven't developed and tasks we'll never accomplish. Unlike children, we are who we are in a way that doesn't seem to allow for much alteration.

In truth, however, our lives began to be shaped and limited much sooner than we would like to admit. We know how important the first few years of our lives are and how they affect what we will think and feel and do for the rest of our lives. But what is becoming clearer is that we're also shaped by the nine months we spend in the womb. For nine months the child is one with its mother, and what she experiences it experiences. The mother's nutrition or lack of it, her health or illness, her emotional well-being or instability all affect the development of the life within her. For those nine months what happens to one happens to the other, but in a different way. The mother can understand what she experiences; the fetus experiences but doesn't understand.

When Fran came to see me, she was pregnant with what would be her third child. Her husband, a policeman, had recently been shot and killed. Overwhelmed by grief, she felt as though she were on an emotional roller-coaster, careening from shock to anger, from remorse to depression. Her parents and sister visited her every day, and her friends, especially a fellow teacher, stood by her. She was comforted by her faith. She had mixed feelings about being pregnant. It reminded her of how she missed her husband and how she had depended on him to be with her at critical times, but it also pulled her through her depression. "There are days I just don't want to get out of bed," she told me. "But I know I have to. I don't feel like eating, but I force myself to eat. I'm not just feeding myself."

In the womb, the fetus felt the impact of Fran's loss, her flinching in pain and tumultuous feelings. Depression triggers a chemical response in the body, and the chemical which flowed through Fran's blood found its way into the blood of the fetus. When Fran climbed aboard the emotional roller-coaster, the fetus went along for the ride. But while Fran could make sense of what was happening to her, the fetus could not. Fran could say, "I feel awful," and know— or be reminded by others—that she herself wasn't awful; the fetus couldn't make the distinction. It wouldn't know what it was feeling, it wouldn't even feel in the same way an adult feels, but it would experience a sense of the awfulness Fran felt. And its sense of awfulness—pre-conscious and inarticulate—would lodge somewhere in its developing mind.

We can't reconstruct what happened to our mothers and, therefore, to us during those first nine months of our lives. We can only imagine that they felt a whole range of emotions—happiness and sadness, delight and apprehension, boredom, anger and love—not all of them, by any means, negative. But undoubtedly they experienced some pain, rejection, and coldness, and what they felt we absorbed and found a place for in us. We have places in us—inaccessible to our conscious minds—where we feel unloved and unlovable, places hollowed out and shaped by what we experienced before we had understanding or awareness. Those places are the chambers and hidden compartments of our boxes. There's nothing in them—no conscious memories—but they're available and ready for occupancy.

From the beginning, there are parts of us that feel damaged. We can't think of any reasons why those parts should be unlovable, precisely because the damage was done before we could reason.

The gods once visited Epimetheus and his wife Pandora. They left the couple with a box, instructing them to safeguard it and never, never to open it. Pandora, knowing her own curiosity and fearing the gods, hid the box deep in the darkest corner of her closet. But she could not resist the temptation or ignore the voices which called to her from the box, and she opened it to peer inside. All the evils of the world—disease, poverty, death—came spewing out, and only after the last one had escaped could she slam the box shut. Sitting on the lid, sobbing, and powerless to summon back the ills she had set loose, she heard another voice, this one clear and sweet, begging to be released. "Oh no," replied Pandora, "I've done enough harm as it is. I'll never open this box again." Still, the voice pleaded, and its words and soft conviction persuaded her to lift the lid one more time. This time a solitary spirit flew out. It was called Hope.

It takes courage—not just curiosity—and all the encouragement others can provide to open the secret box we have pushed into the dim corners of our awareness. It's a risk. But if someone loves us and stands by us through the initial onslaught, we may learn what Pandora discovered: when all hell has broken loose and every demon has been set free, the final word is not despair, but hope.

The journey out of loneliness into love begins when we take the risk of letting another person know us. If we allow someone to stand by us as our accumulated pains and fears come streaming or shrieking or tumbling out of us and if that person does indeed remain with us and love us, then we begin to believe that we can actually be known and loved. Then we can say, "Maybe I'm not so bad after all." It isn't an easy thing to do, letting someone know us through and through, and it doesn't guarantee love. That's why it's a risk. But it's the only way out of loneliness, the only way into love. It's the only way we'll ever be able to hear the sweet voice of hope.

Getting
into
and
out of
Loneliness

We make ourselves lonely because we don't believe that we can be loved. Deep down our poor self-images keep haunting us with the fear that if others truly knew us, they wouldn't love us. And so we develop ways of relating to people which protect us from the rejection we know would face us if they actually saw us as we are. After years and years of repeating these ways of relating, they become habitual.

We develop habits bit by bit, day by day, year by year. Some are quite simple—for example, how we comb our hair or on which wrist we wear our watch—while others involve several elements—like our morning routine of getting out of bed and dressing or the route we follow driving to work. For the most part, habits make our lives easier; they free us from constantly having to rethink things we do over and over again. Our days would be complicated and tiresome without them. Imagine what mornings alone would be like if we had to rethink every option: Are we going to brush our teeth before or after taking a shower? Which hand do we hold the brush in? How do we go about brushing our teeth? Sometime early in childhood we answered all those questions or, more likely, had them answered for us, and with time we incorporated them into a routine we now follow without a second thought. Some habits we learned consciously or, at least, after consideration—like tying our shoes in a certain way or fastening our seat-belts when we're in a car—while others we acquired unconsciously—like fidgeting with some object when we're nervous or assuming a particular position when we lie down to sleep. At the root of our habits lies a fundamentally healthy instinct: the desire to solve a problem, meet a need, accomplish a good. But even if the instinct is positive, the actual habits which result may not be helpful. Many of us, for example, learned that it was good nutrition to eat red meat each day, and so we acquired eating habits which once were thought to be healthy but which are now being questioned. Occasionally our habits lead us to do things we wouldn't have done if we had stopped to consider them. (I've often found myself driving my familiar route to work only to realize somewhere along the way that it's Saturday and I meant to head for the supermarket.) But for the most part habits greatly ease our day.

Since we've learned or acquired habits through repetition, we can change them in much the same way. When I was twenty-eight, I was having my hair cut and the stylist said, "Do you know you're parting your hair on the wrong side?" She informed me that my hair naturally fell the other direction and that I'd have less trouble keeping my cowlick under control if I parted it on the right side instead of the left. It took me a while to change the way I had done something for so many years. Each time I took my comb out, I had to stop myself with a conscious effort and remember to make the part on the right. After repeated efforts, I finally developed a new habit; now I part my hair again without thinking about it. Obviously, some habits are more difficult to change than others. Even when we realize that specific habits are destructive, it's rarely easy to replace them. We all know, for example, that some long-standing habits involving eating and drinking and sexuality seem almost impossible to alter. But we also know that with time, work, and effort, and despite temporary failures and setbacks, we can gradually change our habits.

Our relational patterns are like habits; they're actually clusters of habits. The ways we react to people in particular situations—ways we developed within our families—become ingrained in us through repetition. One event sets off a reaction within us which, in turn, triggers another reaction and possibly another.

Cary, for example, gets so nervous when he's expected to speak in public that his throat tightens and his voice becomes high-pitched and grating. Knowing what he'll sound like even before he speaks, he grows increasingly nervous and begins to shake visibly.

Our relational patterns are rooted in our need to love and to be loved. But since that need is often coupled with the doubt that we can ever really be loved, the patterns which develop, though well-intentioned, are sometimes ineffective and even destructive.

Joan grew up in a family dominated by an authoritarian father. As a child, she had to ask his permission for everything. Years later, as a competent business woman, she found that she was still turning to men, seeking their approval. In turn, she began to resent men and her dependence on them.

Patterns get reinforced not only by repetition but also by the self-perpetuating cycle they set into motion.

Ralph used to become angry and loud when, actually, he was hurting. Since people didn't see his pain—after all, he didn't look hurt—they tended to get angry in return. Then he would become all the angrier and shout all the more, and people would retreat from his rage. The end was worse than the beginning: he dealt with his hurt in such a way that only caused more hurt.

Relational patterns, like habits, can be changed.

Over the years, I've developed a simple, three step process of helping people alter the relational patterns which they've come to see as ineffective. (While the process is simple and straightforward, putting it into effect is not.)

First, it's necessary to recognize the pattern. Like habits which go unnoticed until someone else points them out to us, we assume that the way we relate is the only possible way of doing so. And we often don't even know what we're doing.

After a number of months of being in counseling for

problems she was experiencing at work, Paula began to see her pattern. "When I'm nervous at meetings," she explained, "I tend to talk too much. I don't know why. I suppose it's because my family talks so much and I never felt I was listened to unless I spoke up. Anyway, it's really getting in the way of my job. At meetings when I talk too much, people stop listening to me. Of course, that only makes me feel as though I should say even more."

That's the first step toward change: the recognition of the pattern, "When *this* happens, I tend to do *this*."

The second step in the process is to stop doing whatever it is that we tend to do. Stopping is easier said than done. Our patterns are so deeply ingrained in us that they seem the only natural and reasonable thing to do.

Paula clearly saw how her pattern led to a frustrating cycle of talking too much, feeling ignored, and talking even more to get people's attention. When I first suggested that she consider not talking at meetings, however, she immediately reacted in anger: "You're telling me to sit there like a kid and not be heard from." I explained how she had developed the ability to express herself so well that she didn't have to worry about losing that skill. She needed to develop other skills, like listening, but in order to do so she had to stop relying on the one skill which she so readily used.

I tell people who are trying to change their patterns that at the first moment they realize their pattern is kicking into gear they should imagine a large, blinking red light. The light has one message: Stop! It tells them they must stop dead in their tracks and *not do* what they're most inclined to do. If they try to reason with their pattern, they're lost.

Paula agreed to try my experiment, although I could see she wasn't convinced. She returned the next session to report that her efforts had failed. "I know I agreed not to talk at meetings," she started, "and I really can see how talking so much is self-defeating. But at this last meeting, I simply had to say something. I mean, I couldn't just sit there and let a measure get voted on without saying what had to be said." I asked her what happened. "Well," she admitted, "people disregarded what I said. But don't you see? I had to speak up. Just this time. In general, I agree I shouldn't talk so much." Once we begin to reason with our patterns, they will always win. They have all the convincing weight of experience on their side, and they can offer a host of reasons to persuade us to keep relying on them. They are the tried and true ways we have always used to relate to people. And even when we acknowledge their deficiencies, they still offer the comfort of familiarity.

The third and final step is only possible after we've come to a complete stop. Then and only then can we start doing what is directly counter to what we typically do.

Initially in order to please me, Paula agreed not to speak at any meeting unless someone directly asked for her opinion. "At first," she reported, "no one even looked in my direction when we were discussing an issue I'd spoken against many times in the past. I thought I was going to burst. You know what happened, though? Someone else raised the same objections I had noted before. I didn't even know he agreed with me. I didn't say a thing the entire meeting. That sure felt strange. And you could tell people were thinking something was wrong with me. Next meeting, same thing. There was a pause when everyone was expecting me to say something and I didn't. I almost had to bite my tongue to keep from saying what I thought. It's hard work, but I can already see it's what I need to do."

The process is the same for everyone who wants to change: *recognize* the pattern, *stop* doing what we typically do, *start* doing what runs counter to it. Obviously, patterns vary from person to person and what people must do to change them likewise varies. Not everyone, for example, should refuse to talk at meetings until asked for an opinion; some people, in fact, should make themselves speak up even when they feel they have nothing worthwhile to contribute.

We've developed our relational patterns over years, and

it's foolish to think we can change them easily or quickly. But we can change them.

When our relational patterns are rooted in a poor self-image, they become what I call patterns of loneliness. I believe that there are four general patterns.

Each of the patterns is rooted in the basic premise of a poor self-image: "If you really knew me, you wouldn't love me." Each one grows out of a fundamental choice: either to be known (and, therefore, not loved) or to be loved (and, therefore, not known). And each one blossoms into a fully developed and self-perpetuating cycle. A particular skill or basic instinct nourishes each pattern. In itself, the skill or instinct is healthy and life-giving; but it has become destructive since its growth has stunted the development of other necessary skills and instincts.

In the following chapters, I'll describe the four patterns. I'll analyze how they spring from a poor self-image and how they evolve into a complex and seemingly reasonable, though self-defeating, system. Finally, I'll show how the patterns of loneliness can be recognized, stopped, and refashioned into patterns of love.

The
Romancer

*R*omancers are the Don Quixotes of life, stirring the waters of emotion and leaving in their wake a swirl of passion. They set off on the endless quest for Dulcinea, their one abiding love who will faithfully return their affection. Romeo and Juliet were Romancers. So was Beethoven.

A Contemporary Romancer

Anyone who knew Martin through grade and high school certainly knew that he was shy. He was likeable but quiet. His classmates called him a dreamer. In a way they were right because Martin lived in a world of his own. He cried at movies and loved the tales of King Arthur and the Round Table. Although he had strong feelings, he held them out of sight. Martin fell in love regularly, although the people he loved never knew it. If the "right" girl came along, he reasoned, she would know his love without having to be told and she would love him. He yearned to be loved but kept searching for this special someone.

In college he rarely dated. He didn't understand how other men in his dormitory could bounce from one girl to another. Then, during his junior year, Martin met Helen. It was instant love. From the very first moment he knew she was special, not like the other women he had loved. She was aware of his hidden feelings. She didn't laugh at his romantic notions. She was affectionate, attractive, and popular. Martin felt like the luckiest man in the world to be loved by such a woman. Helen was the one he had been waiting for all his life. Emotions held back for years now overflowed their boundaries.

At first Helen was bemused and touched by Martin's

dramatic and constant show of affection: flowers and notes and late night talks when he poured his heart out to her. Still, she felt crowded and, at times, overwhelmed. It was all too much. She told him finally that she needed to move more slowly.

During their senior year they shared an apartment. Martin was delighted. As last his dreams were coming true. He fantasized all the more about how happy they would be once they were married.

One day, without leaving a note or giving an explanation, Helen moved out of the apartment. Martin was stunned. He was certain that something had happened to her. He searched frantically for a day and a half; it was like a nightmare. Finally he found her in their favorite restaurant, but she was with another man. "I'm sorry, Martin," was all she had to say. It was unbearable.

At first Martin couldn't believe that Helen wouldn't be back. He waited and waited but gradually realized he was waiting for nothing. He became despondent. He mourned the death of love and cursed her fickleness. He swore he'd never fall in love again, at least not with a woman like Helen. In his heart he blamed himself for picking the wrong woman. "Never again," he told himself. "Never again."

Still depressed, Martin needed to talk to someone. He thought of Carl, a man he had met the previous year. Carl was quiet and accepting. He listened as Martin recounted the sad story of his all too brief love. Carl didn't speak much and he didn't ask much from Martin; he was content just to listen. He was there whenever Martin needed a shoulder to cry on.

After graduation Martin was hired by a bank. He found himself attracted to a woman who worked with him. At first he held back, but then he reasoned that she was nothing like Helen. She was plain, steady, and intelligent, not at all the kind of person to sweep Martin off his feet. Still, she was intuitive, and she seemed to sense the depth of his feelings. Since she had recently broken up with a man she'd lived with for two years, she was sympathetic to Martin's pain. She knew what it was like to be disappointed in love. They liked the same kind of movies, and before long they were dating.

Martin was drawn to Jeannette's warmth, her sense of humor, and her appreciation of the dramatic, but he felt something was missing. He didn't experience the same sort of emotional charge around her that he had around Helen. As much as he resented Helen for forsaking him, Martin had idealized her; for him, she was still the perfect woman. In his mind he continually compared Jeannette to her.

When Jeannette and Martin began discussing marriage, he felt strangely ambivalent. He wanted more than anything to be married and he was tired of living alone; but he also thought that when the time came he'd feel more confident and alive. They married on the anniversary of their first date.

Marriage wasn't what Martin had expected. He thought things would somehow be different, happier and less routine. He was disappointed that Jeannette continued working, and although he didn't say anything to her, he had imagined that she should stay at home and care for the house. When Jeannette became pregnant, Martin grew excited at the prospect of being a father. He was pleased when Jeannette took a leave from work after their son was born. But just as things were getting better, something else began going wrong. Initially it was like a whisper inside of him, a whisper he tried to ignore, but it wouldn't be silent. He was jealous. Jeannette seemed to love the baby more than she loved him. He kept asking himself how he could be jealous of a baby, of his own son.

Martin found himself thinking more and more of Helen and all the good times they had enjoyed together. As his sexual relationship with Jeannette became less fulfilling, Martin even fantasized about Helen in place of Jeannette. Although he hadn't seen Helen since he walked out of that restaurant, the thought of her was filling more and more of his life. What would happen if he and Helen met again?

Jeannette earned a real estate license and began working at home. When she had evening appointments, Martin looked after their son. Although they needed the money, Martin felt that Jeannette was spending too much time with her work or with the baby. He felt neglected and became progressively more angry—angry with his wife, with her job, with the baby, but mostly angry with himself for being angry. He tried to swallow his anger, but the harder he tried, the more withdrawn he became. He retreated further and further into a world of his own, a fantasy world. He spoke less and less.

What Martin didn't say to Jeannette in words still got communicated. She knew she fell short of his expectations, and she grew tired of living with his unspoken disapproval. One day she moved herself and her son to her mother's house and left a note for Martin. They met several times afterward to discuss the particulars but she had little doubt about what needed to be done. She filed for divorce and won custody of their son.

Living in an apartment, Martin was numb, confused and angry—all at the same time. It was as though he were re-living a nightmare: abandoned and alone once again.

Although Martin had lost touch with Carl over the years, he was able to locate him and re-establish contact. Carl seemed the same as always, ready to listen and offer sympathy. Martin wondered why the women he loved couldn't be as faithful as Carl.

Afraid that he might never find the right woman, Martin resolved not to let his feelings rule his life. He promised himself that he'd be more careful about falling in love the next time. He knew there was a woman waiting for him, the woman of his dreams who would love him faithfully. But he also knew that he was twenty-eight. Perhaps the opportunity of finding this person had passed him by. Driven by this fear, he pushed caution aside and intensified his search. But the more eagerly he pursued, the more quickly the person backed away from him. Several attempts ended in failure and after each Martin felt alone and lonely.

Whenever Martin was in love, he called Carl to boast about her qualities and to assure his friend that this time he'd found the woman he'd been looking for all along. And each time she left, Martin called Carl for sympathy.

The Loneliness Pattern

The poor self-image of Romancers sets off a spiraling pattern of loneliness.

Although in their hearts they fear they can never be known and loved, they hope there's one person in the world who will truly know them and love them anyway. "There's someone," they believe, "who will love me perfectly—without conditions or reservations and for all time. And when I find that person and when I'm loved in that way, I'll be made whole. Then I'll be happy."

It's a self-defeating and self-perpetuating cycle. Feeling bad about themselves, they seek one person who will meet all their emotional and relational needs. They become over-possessive. There is no one who can live up to their expectations, no one who can give them the total, unwavering, and constant acceptance they long for. When the people they love show the least sign of hesitancy or half-heartedness, Romancers feel rejected. Being rejected confirms their poor self-image and the cycle begins again.

Romancers live in a fantasy world where ideals are the law of the land. In the sanctuary of their imaginations, everything is as it should be: clean and neat. There is no ambiguity, no need for compromise, no reason to settle for anything short of perfection. Love is a wonderful and unwavering feeling, freely exchanged; once given, it can't be lost or diminished. When people love each other, they're never angry or lukewarm. They're happy all the time.

In this fantasy world of their own making, Romancers fare no better than others. Who can measure up to a system of absolutes where there is only good or evil, perfection or failure, love or rejection? No one lives up to their ideals, least of all themselves. They are constantly disappointed with others and they are constantly disappointed with themselves. Their fantasy world is really one of disappointment.

Most of us have ideals. They animate, inspire and challenge us. Without them we would become disheartened, complacent, or cynical. But Romancers have extreme ideals. They set goals hopelessly beyond their reach and crowd their lives with impossible "shoulds." These over-inflated ideals insure failure. Neither they nor others could possibly meet their expectations. Using such over-inflated ideals as a measurement of success, it's no wonder Romancers are never satisfied with themselves.

Romancers constantly seek the over-idealized in themselves and in the ones they love, and they inevitably fail to find what they seek. Their failure robs them of self-confidence and reinforces their low self-esteem. In turn, the more inadequate they feel, the more compelled they are to find someone whose total and all-embracing love will make up for what is missing in their lives.

Romancers live with extremes and they don't know what to make of the normal day-to-day sort of feelings. Ambivalence (contradictory emotions existing side by side) and nuance (the subtle shades of distinctions between feelings) often elude or confuse them. They swing from highs to lows. When they're in love, everything is wonderful. When they're alone, their world falls apart. It's hard for Romancers to live with the middle range of emotions.

Martin came in to see me after his divorce and following a series of unsuccessful relationships. He described himself as a failure.

"No one loves me," he complained, "and I can't say I blame them. Sometimes I feel as though I'm a fraud. I want so much to be loved, I'll do almost anything. But it's as though I'm selling myself. And I don't even believe in the product.''

Family Dynamics

The Romancers' patterns don't happen accidently. They begin to form bit by bit from their earliest years.

Even as little children, Romancers felt a need for more love than they received. It isn't that they weren't loved and loved a lot. It's just that they wanted to be loved more, and it seemed that someone else always received the love they were looking for. Sometimes it was a brother or sister, sometimes a neighbor, sometimes a cousin.

When Romancers think of their families, their own ideals trip them up. According to their ideals, love never fails or falters; it's total and absolute. Romancers don't know what to make of their parents' love for them. Though it was genuine, it wasn't perfect. To them, being loved imperfectly translates into being loved not at all, and yet they know their parents loved them.

Romancers feel a great deal of ambivalence about their parents. They can't bring themselves to admit that their parents were anything less than perfect. At the same time, they realize that their parents didn't love them as they should have. Romancers are often confused about their own feelings for parents and family.

Martin described his parents as hard-working and successful. They owned a small market and ran it themselves. They were affectionate, and although they didn't readily show their emotions, Martin had little reason to doubt their love for him. He did, however, doubt himself. He always felt as though he were a disappointment to them. Martin had an older brother, Jim, who was constantly held up to him as an example.

"Jim was everything I knew I should be," Martin reflected. "Good looking. Successful at school. Into sports. He was the only one my parents would trust to run the store when they were away."

"What's it like to have a brother like that?"

"It's just great. I guess I should resent him. I mean, I was always being compared to him. And nothing I ever did was as good as what he had done or could have done. But, you know, I could see why everyone liked him so much. He really is as good as everyone says. He's even a good brother. How could I resent him? I'm grateful he's my brother. But . . . ."

"But?"

"But I can't help it. I resent him. It's crazy, I know. He's a hero, he really is. I admire him."

"You admire him?"

"I admire him and I resent him. He's the person I always wanted to be."

Heroes play an important role in the fantasy world of Romancers. They're the embodiment of Romancers' ideals, the living proof that perfection is possible. If only Romancers try harder, they can be like their heroes—perfect in every way.

Romancers don't actually love their heroes; they admire them from afar. Heroes have to be kept at a distance, since once they're seen up close their flaws become apparent. Romancers also resent their heroes. They see them as constant reminders of their own inadequacies. Caught in the dilemma of resenting someone they admire, Romancers feel guilty.

As Romancers grow up, their parents and family communicate a subtle (and sometimes not so subtle) message: "You're not enough—not good enough, not smart enough, not successful enough." They lack something. They may never have been told clearly what it was they lacked, but they knew something was missing. And they suspected that their lack explained why others, especially their parents, didn't love them as much as they wanted to be loved.

It's this early family message ("you're not enough") that sets into gear the two major dynamics of the Romancer pattern: their ideals (what should be) and their search for someone who will love them and make up for what they lack.

Romancers as Seen from the Outside

During one of our sessions, Martin concluded a stinging assessment of one of his broken relationships, saying, "She's just like all the others."

"Who is?" I asked, "Helen or Jeannette?"

"No, no. Not them, although they're the same, too. I was talking about Marcie, the last one who left me."

"You know," I confessed, "sometimes I get confused."

"What do you mean?"

"Sometimes I don't know who you're talking about. There are a number of different women involved, but after a while they all begin to sound alike—at least as I hear you talk about them." I paused and let him reflect for a moment. "At first, they're enchanting, lovely, and everything you've always dreamed about. Then something happens and they become petty, angry, and thoughtless. Without shedding a tear, they leave you."

"That's exactly what happens. Every time."

"I wonder what they would have to say."

Until now, I've been examining the Romancer Pattern from the vantage point of the Romancers. Now I'd like to change my approach and look at Romancers and their ways of relating from the perspective of those who love them.

Being loved by a Romancer is at first a delightful experience.

If you've ever been loved by a Romancer, you know

what it's like to feel special. You know what it's like to be the center of someone else's world. Romancers see only the good in you. They praise your virtues and seem oblivious to your faults. Romancers are constantly searching for their one true love, the person who embodies all that is noble and beautiful, and they've found what they seek in you. You are their Romeo, their Juliet. And who wouldn't enjoy being cast as the romantic lead in a dramatic tale?

It's thrilling to be loved by Romancers, to be caught up in the swirl of their passion. Everyone dreams of being loved by someone without question or qualification, and you've found such a person.

With time, however, the joy of being loved by a Romancer turns to disappointment and resentment.

You begin to realize that they love you not as you are but as they imagine you to be. While you were initially happy having your faults overlooked, you begin to wish you could just be yourself, warts and all. You grow tired of having to hide your ambivalence, doubts and fears, anger, and anything else that's messy and unbecoming of a romantic hero or heroine. You wonder if you've really been loved at all. Did they love you or their image of you? You feel cheated.

At about the same time that you're becoming disillusioned with the way Romancers love you, they are also becoming disillusioned. In spite of their best efforts to see you through the rose-colored glasses of their ideals, they can't sustain their illusions. They begin to notice your faults. They see things in the extreme, all or nothing. Previously they didn't see your faults at all; now that's all they see. And since they have difficulty acknowledging and expressing their own negative feelings, they hold in all their anger and disappointment. They may think they're concealing their judgments and their growing resentment, but you know what they're thinking. Their feelings toward you change dramatically, and where once you could do no wrong, now you can do no right. They let you know in so many ways that you don't measure up. You're not the romantic fulfillment of all their dreams. When they discover you're not really Romeo or Juliet, they feel betrayed. You let them down.

On the one hand, you feel duped; you thought they actually loved you and, as it turns out, they were only in love with their own idealization. On the other hand, you feel judged, as though it's your fault you're not perfect. You may try, at first, to talk with them about your feelings and theirs and about what they're communicating to you, but you eventually give up in resignation. Afraid of conflict and their own unspoken feelings of failure, they turn away from you. They retreat into their own fantasy world, and you feel isolated.

Frustrated and hurt, you decide to leave. But now you're really caught in a bind. In your mind, you're simply acknowledging what seems patently obvious: the relationship has ended. If you were to assign responsibility for its ending, you'd probably assume some yourself and lay some of it at the feet of the Romancer. They, however, act shocked, as though they had no idea things had fallen apart. They assume the role of the innocent victim, the one whose extravagant love was, in the end, unrequited. Once you were the romantic lead. Now you're the heartless villain.

"Tell me about Carl," I said to Martin during one of our sessions.

"He's a great guy. He's always there when I need him. He listens. He cares. He lets me rant and rave. He's never disappointed me. He doesn't laugh at the things I do. Well, he does laugh. But he's not laughing at me, if you know what I mean."

"You've just told me all the things he does for you. I asked you about him."

"What do you mean?"

"He's there when you need him. He listens. He cares. He laughs. It's all what he does for you. I asked you what he's like and all you told me is what he does for you. And even then you didn't say a word about what you do for him."

Romancers don't focus much attention on their friends. They concentrate their energies into pursuing lovers, and they devote little thought to developing and maintaining friendships.

If you've ever had Romancers for friends, you've probably learned to take them with a grain of salt. You may find them amusing, since they're people of extremes. At one moment they're boasting to you about their latest love, using the most exaggerated terms. And the next time you see them, they're in grief, betrayed once again by the cruelty of life and the fickleness of love. You don't see them much in between the starting and the ending of their affairs. And you've certainly learned not to count on them for your own emotional support. You may find yourself feeling used. They're around only when they need you, and it's clear that they're only using you to get what they want until they can get it from someone they value more.

After a while you give up expecting much consistency from the Romancers in your life. They're your friends when they're in need. And while you may continue to like them, you don't invest much of your emotional energy into your friendship with them. In turn, the distance they feel from you only serves to reinforce their fantasy that only one person can ever meet their need for love.

Summary: The Romancer Pattern of Loneliness

No two Romancers are the same. By nature, they would resist being clumped into a group with other people. They would insist, rightly, that they are unique and their experiences are unlike those of Martin. Still, the Romancer Pattern threads through all the variations.

Romancers live in a fantasy world, constantly seeking someone who will sweep them off their feet and save them from the mess that is within them. They feel inadequate and unworthy of love, but they hope against hope that there's one person truly capable of loving them and of making them worthy.

Romancers compare what is with what exists in their fantasies, and they're inevitably dissatisfied. Some Romancers compare their present relationships to former ones which they've recreated according to their ideals. Some Romancers have never experienced any love which comes close to their ideal, so they construct an ideal of a future relationship, and they use this ideal future as the standard by which to judge their present relationships.

Romancers doubt themselves and their ability to sustain a loving relationship. They're all too aware of their failed attempts. No one has ever loved them the way they want to be loved.

Their poor self-image spurs them on to love in a way that's doomed to fail, and their failures confirm their reasons for feeling bad about themselves.

The Romancer's Way from Loneliness to Love

The main skill Romancers have developed is the ability to fall in love. They're willing to risk. And while risking isn't the whole of love, it's the beginning of it. Romancers make themselves vulnerable. They pour themselves into love without counting the cost or protecting themselves from the inevitable pain of loss.

The ability to fall in love and to lose themselves in the experience of being loved is the gift Romancers possess. And it's a gift to be valued.

Gifts, even valued gifts, become problems when they're relied on too much. Romancers fall into a self-perpetuating pattern of loneliness because they have over-developed their one skill—that of falling in love—and haven't supplemented it with other necessary skills.

To work their way out of loneliness, Romancers must

counter-balance the one skill they've mastered so well. They must develop other skills.

From Idealism to Realism

Romancers must develop a critical eye. They tend to see things as they want them to be and to be blind to what falls short of their idealistic standards. They have to look long and hard to see things as they are, not as they wish they were.

While Romancers might think that becoming critical is cold and heartless, it is in fact more compassionate than their typical approach.

Romancers may shudder at the thought of needing to become critical, equating criticism with negativity. But, in fact, seeing things as they are is more compassionate and loving than trying to make them fit pre-conceived ideals of how things should be. A healthy dose of realism would help Romancers accept people—including themselves—as they are: not wholly good or irredeemably bad, but an uneven mixture of both; with strengths and weaknesses, gifts and liabilities existing side by side in a sometimes uneasy truce. Love—real love, not romanticized love—of others and of self becomes possible only with acceptance.

They must let go of the illusion that people are perfect or that they can ever become perfect if they only tried hard enough. Romancers, themselves, aren't perfect and they never will be. Furthermore, no one else is perfect. No one they loved in the past was perfect and no one they meet in the future will be perfect either.

"I know I blame others," Martin said, beginning one of our sessions, "and I know it does me no good. So I'm kind of hesitant to say this, but I can't help thinking I wouldn't be the way I am if it hadn't been for my parents. I'm not blaming them—really, I'm not. But can you tell me

72

why I keep feeling I wouldn't be having these problems if they had been better parents?"

"Sounds as if you're dealing with them exactly the same way they dealt with you."

"What do you mean?"

"You keep telling me how you never lived up to their expectations, how they always wanted you to be better than you were, how they couldn't accept you for yourself. Well, it sounds to me as though you're doing the same thing to them. 'If only they had been better parents' is how you said it. Isn't 'better' the problem?"

"I'm not sure I understand."

"Can you show me how the way you're dealing with them is any different from the way they dealt with you?"

"I guess I see what you're getting at," he admitted after some reflection. "I was never good enough for them. And now they're not good enough for me."

"You seem to be judging them by standards that you admit didn't work when they used them on you."

"You're right. I didn't like it when they wanted me to be more than I was. And yet I keep trying to make them be more than they are. But what else can I do?"

"Have you ever thought about who they actually are instead of who they ought to be?"

Martin became reflective and began to speak as though I weren't in the room. For the first time I heard him describe his parents as caring people. They were fair and hard-working, but more than that they were consistently with him when he needed them. Often they didn't understand what he was going through, but they still remained supportive. His mother, who always called him weekly, took to calling him even more frequently during those periods when he was depressed. Although his father always complained about the nuisance of writing letters, he wrote to Martin on a regular basis. "My father, of all people," Martin remarked, "never forgets my birthday." His parents made him feel guilty about not visiting them as often as he should, and when he was home they made him feel guilty about not being more successful at the bank. "The funny thing is, despite the fact that they never seem completely satisfied," Martin concluded, "I know they're proud of me. They really are."

"Sounds as if they're pretty decent people after all."

"Well, you know, I guess they are."

"What you just did," I reflected, "is to deal with your parents not as they should be, but as they are. And that worked out pretty well. I wonder what would happen if you did the same for yourself."

Over the next several sessions, I noticed a gradual change in the way Martin talked about people. He described his boss, his brother, a woman he had met at work, in realistic terms. They weren't villains or heroes. They were flesh and blood people. Likewise, Martin began to talk about himself with more realism. He accurately assessed his strengths and weaknesses, and he admitted his faults without unduly criticizing himself or blowing them out of proportion. He began to speak of himself as someone of worth.

From Extremes to Moderation

Romancers must learn to live in the middle range of emotions and relationships.

Romancers are passionate people who feel things deeply. They know what it's like to be infatuated, despairing, joyful, and miserable. As artists of the emotional life, they've mastered all the primary colors, the bold ones that stand out and catch people's eyes. They need to experiment with the subtler shades of emotions, the less striking hues which add nuance and depth, the in-between kinds of feelings like happiness, contentment, concern, regret, pleasure, boredom.

I began one of our sessions observing that something had changed.

"What's changed?" Martin asked.

"You have. For the past several weeks you've been talking about problems at work, your parents, the woman you're thinking about asking for a date, and it sounds as if you're doing O.K."

"Well, that's how I feel. O.K. I'm not feeling great. I'm not feeling awful. I'm just feeling O.K."

"What's changed?"

"What do you mean?"

"Well, it doesn't seem to me as if much has changed in your life. You're still divorced. You still have the same parents you always had and they're basically the same people they always were. Your job hasn't changed. The things in your life haven't changed much. But you've changed."

"I don't know. Maybe it's my attitude. This is going to sound stupid, but I think it's O.K. to feel O.K. In the past I thought something was wrong if I didn't feel terrific, if my day wasn't wonderful. Now life just seems to go on, some highs, some lows, but no real peaks or valleys."

"Is that a problem?"

"Well, I have to admit, once in a while I'd love to feel the old passionate feelings. You know, the knocked-off-my-feet-by-love kind of feelings. But I don't miss for a moment the despair and depression that always seemed to follow. And these days I find myself enjoying small things. It used to be that things had to stand out in bold relief for me to notice. Now I'm feeling more. I'm not feeling more intensely, I'm just feeling more feelings, like being satisfied with something I've done or appreciating it when my boss says something nice to me."

Just as Romancers tend to relish their passionate feelings while downplaying their more ordinary ones, so they tend to devote all of their energy to the more significant relationships while slighting the less important ones. Specifically, they focus all of their attention on their lovers—former, current, and future—and pay little heed to friends and associates. By fixating on one relationship at a time, they ensure its demise. Cultivating more relationships of various intensities would help them break out of this pattern. If some of their needs for affection and attention were met by a variety of people, they would feel less pressure to have all those needs met by one.

Martin noticed that he still tended to focus too much attention on a woman he worked with, so I encouraged him to examine his other relationships. We considered various possibilities, and he decided to join a couple of business friends in their weekly bowling excursions. Playing volleyball on Sunday afternoons with a church group led him to volunteer one Saturday each month at a soup kitchen. Although some people still seemed hesitant around him, due to his past pattern of becoming involved with them only to withdraw at a later date, he found that many of his relationships deepened. He gained an added sense of self-confidence. He remained concerned about finding the one woman who would meet all of his needs, but since many of his needs were being met by himself and by his new friends he became less desperate in his search.

From Dependence to Independence

Romancers believe they are incomplete and can't stand on their own. They seek someone whose love will make them whole. The more Romancers assure themselves of their own competence and independence, the more they will be free to enter into healthy relationships. When they desperately need someone else, they must stop and recognize their own gifts and talents. They're competent people, and they can stand on their own. It's not a question of competency, but a question of valuing what they do. They need to claim their accomplishments and feel good about the things they do so they don't overburden their relationships, especially their primary ones.

As time went on Martin began seeing me less and less frequently, and it became clear that our time of working together was coming to a close. During one of our last sessions, he said, "I really want to thank you."

"For what?"

"For all you've done for me."

"What do you mean?"

"Stop kidding around. You know precisely what I mean. I've changed so much. I'm not going to say I'm perfect, but I'm lots better off. And it's all because of you."

"I don't understand how you can do that."

"Do what?"

"Give me all that power. I saw you once a week, sometimes less. For an hour a week. And I did all this work? You're the one who worked. You're the one who made the changes. I've stood by and watched as you struggled and agonized and kicked and screamed and took responsibility for your life. But you're the one who did it. I couldn't have done it for you even if I'd wanted to."

"I guess I was making you my new hero," he said, laughing. "Well, let me try that again. Thanks for being with me as I took charge of my life and put it back together again."

The
Pleaser

*P*leasers are fun people. They're gregarious and out-going, quick to tell jokes, and happiest when other people are happy. Charming and successful, Pleasers are friends with everyone and want everyone to be friends with them.

A Contemporary Pleaser

Barbara was attractive. Everyone said so, but she always thought of herself as plain. "Wholesome" was the word she used. Her father was a physician, and his profession kept him occupied most of the time. Her mother was also busy taking care of five children. Barbara was fourth in line; she had an older brother and two older sisters as well as a younger sister. It was a close-knit family. She knew her parents loved her and were proud of her. She and her brother and sisters all had a happy childhood.

When Barbara was five years old, she became seriously ill. Her mother spent a great deal of time caring for her. In the years following her recovery, she missed the attention her mother had given her. She felt as though she had become less special in her mother's eyes and wondered what she had done wrong. She worked very hard to regain the attention she had once enjoyed.

Barbara's mother encouraged all her children to succeed at school and frequently said, "Make me proud of you." She was careful not to compare the children to each other, but they all knew the best way to win her approval was to bring home good reports from school. One day when Barbara was in the third grade, she came home in tears and told her mother that she had received a "B" on a class project. Her mother held her in her arms and reassured her, "Don't you worry about it. I know you can do better. If you work a little harder, I'm sure you can get an 'A' next time." Her mother died when Barbara was in the sixth grade, but she never forgot those words.

In high school Barbara made the honor roll every semester. In her third year, she was elected class president. She had a talent for music, and she excelled at playing the piano. As a senior she edited the yearbook and became a national merit scholar. Although she rarely dated, she was popular and had many friends. She enjoyed teaming up with other people on a common project, and they found her easy to work with. When she was the valedictorian at the graduation ceremony, her father told her how proud he was of her and that he loved her very much.

She entered a small Catholic college with a full scholarship. Her college career nearly duplicated her earlier successes. If anything, she was even more popular. She sang and played the piano, worked for the college newspaper, and served on the student senate. While she was well-liked and had an active social life, she always thought of her father, brother and sisters as her closest friends. She graduated *magna cum laude* and was a member of Phi Beta Kappa.

About that time, her brother entered the seminary to study for the priesthood. She was surprised because she had secretly considered becoming a nun.

Barbara went on to graduate school, earned a doctorate in nursing, and obtained a position at a Catholic hospital run by the same community of nuns who taught at her alma mater. She was a popular administrator. People liked the way she made them feel important.

As the years went on, her thoughts of becoming a nun persisted. To leave all she was doing was a great risk, but she finally decided to "give it a try." Like everything else Barbara tried, it was a great success. She became an ideal nun. She worked hard and gained the respect of the other sisters in her religious community. There was one area, however, that bothered her. She felt she had not succeeded in regard to spiritual devotions. Although she attended Mass daily and was faithful to community prayer, she never felt particularly close to God. She consoled herself, thinking that while others may be closer to God, she was one of his hardest workers. She wondered, whenever she slowed down enough to reflect, whether God was as pleased with her as others were.

Barbara's talents as a hospital administrator led her to a new position as the director of personnel for her religious community. There were too few sisters and too many openings, and she was caught between the needs of the institutions and the needs of the women she represented. No one knew how she managed to keep everyone happy. Following this she was asked and agreed to return to hospital administration. She was appointed the CEO of a large medical center operated by her religious community. It was a challenging position which she handled well for twelve years.

Throughout this time Barbara's family was as supportive as ever. She remained close to her father and to her brother and sisters and to their families. She was, in fact, the favorite aunt of her nieces and nephews.

After twenty years in religious life, she was elected on the first ballot as the provincial leader of her community.

On the occasion of her twenty-fifth anniversary as a nun, her family insisted on hosting a celebration. She had so many friends who meant so much to her that she had difficulty limiting her party list to a hundred and twenty-five of her most special friends. It was a marvelous affair, and being surrounded by all the people who loved her made her ecstatic.

Three days afterward her father died of a heart attack. She was numb. She had lost the most precious person in her life, a person who loved her dearly just because of who she was. Losing him made her realize there was no one else in her life who really loved her in the same way. She experienced the loss of her father much more deeply than she had the loss of her mother. She felt even more isolated as people reached out to console her. For the first time in her life she wished she had a family of her own. This feeling intensified as she cleaned out her father's home and put it on the market to sell.

Barbara found herself bored at work, unable to concentrate. One day she began crying uncontrollably, as she had done in the third grade. This time, though, there was no one to hold her and to reassure her as her mother had done. When she started missing Mass and community prayers, the sisters in her religious community knew something was wrong but they didn't know what to do. Barbara sensed their concern, but her inability to let them help her made her realize that she only knew how to be of help to others. She admitted for the first time that she was lonely. All of her success and popularity seemed so shallow. She felt that she had wasted her life on things that didn't matter.

The Pleaser Dynamic

Pleasers believe they can compensate for their poor self-image by winning the approval of others.

They're competent and hard-working and generally so successful that they appear to have little reason to feel bad about themselves. Although often quite intelligent, their ceaseless interest in people and engagement in projects keep them from realizing how they use their accomplishments and success to earn approval. Activity numbs the pain and helps them not to face the loneliness of their flourishing but shallow life-style.

Pleasers have learned over the years that their accomplishments and what they do for others will earn them approval. They work hard to make others feel good about themselves, hoping in turn that others will appreciate them. It's generally a very successful system. People do enjoy the attention and concern shown them by Pleasers and do praise them for all their work.

Pleasers don't relate deeply. They're friendly and well-liked, and while they are well known by many people they're not known well by anyone. They relate to others in terms of what they can do for them.

Approval is the mainspring of the Pleasers' dynamic. Their need for approval sets the whole unconscious pattern of Pleasers in operation and keeps it running. Their poor self-image makes them work to earn approval; and when they receive approval for what they do, they feel the need to work all the harder. They feel affirmed by the praise they receive but never loved.

The approval that sustains Pleasers isn't the same thing as love. It doesn't touch them deeply enough to make them feel good about who they are, but it does satisfy part of their appetite. Their need for approval is like a bad diet. It allows them to survive. It keeps them from thriving, even though they look vibrant and alive. It allows them to deny the depth of their own needs and from realizing how superficial most of their relationships are. It makes them satisfied but never happy, appreciated but never loved. It keeps them lonely.

Pleasers may never realize how lonely they are. If they work hard enough and continue being successful and if others consistently praise them and give them the affirmation they seek, Pleasers are capable of surviving for all their lives. Often, however, a crisis puts a halt to their pattern and makes them face the depth of their loneliness.

Families play a decisive role in the development of the Pleaser's pattern.

We don't choose the families we're born into. And especially in our early years we have little, if any, say in choosing the important people in our lives. Parents, brothers and sisters, grandparents, aunts and uncles—all are what I call "givens." They're the people who make decisions for us; they're the ones whose lives shape ours. Given relationships may be close and meaningful or distant and harmful. They may be constant and faithful or painfully inconsistent and unreliable. As children we had no choice in the matter; these were the people who helped to shape our lives, these were the models who taught us about loving and being loved.

As we mature and take responsibility for our own lives, we must make choices about our given relationships. We must, in a sense, choose what to do with what has been given us. Some of us leave our parents altogether and never speak with them again. Some break away for a while, only to return later and build a new and more equal relationship. The choices we make differ from person to person; they may be more or less realistic, more or less loving. But if, at least, we learn to make a choice, even if it's a bad one, we then have the capacity to remake it.

If we don't make choices about our given relationships, our families, we will be severely hampered in making other choices about relationships in our lives.

That's the problem Pleasers run into.

Pleasers do make choices, in a sense. They choose to value their families and continue relating to them as they did when they were children. In effect, they choose not to choose. They maintain their given relationships exactly as they always were.

As children we all tried to please our parents and families, hoping to win their love and approval. We learned from our earliest years that meeting their expectations and making them feel good brought us affection and attention. But there comes a time when we must risk losing their approval—risk losing their love—if we're ever to become our own person.

Pleasers don't take that risk. They don't grow beyond their childhood patterns of pleasing others. Concerned about living up to other people's expectations, they don't make choices based on their sense of who they are.

Pleasers grow up remaining dependent on the nurture and support of their parents and other given relationships. They never fully risk the kind of challenging and assertive behavior necessary to establish adult relationships. Their families are often close and loving, but they can't provide the needed depth of intimacy that other mature relationships can.

Pleasers have learned from their family how to win approval, not how to risk love.

Barbara's mother and father both reinforced her pattern of pleasing, although they did so in different ways. Her mother clearly rewarded her accomplishments and encouraged her to keep working hard. When Barbara brought home a good report card—and it was always a good one—her mother praised her, saying, "That's terrific. You make me so proud of you. I know you can do even better next time." In her well-intentioned effort to encourage her daughter to be the best she could be, Barbara's mother inadvertently fostered a cycle of working, achieving, and working even harder.

Her father was a gentle and unobtrusive man, too busy with his medical practice to give much attention to his children. He didn't actively encourage Barbara's work, and on occasions he even told her directly that he loved her for who she was and not just for what she did. Those occasions, however, were infrequent and mostly linked to times when she succeeded in a spectacular way (being the valedictorian, earning a doctorate, being elected provincial of her community).

Her mother died before Barbara could rebel against her expectations, and her father's love was so comfortable and important to her that she never did anything to put it in jeopardy. Both her parents loved her and sincerely wanted the best for her. But Barbara's dependence on their love and her unwillingness to change her way of relating to them kept her from learning how to take the risks which are necessary to break out of a pattern that ultimately fosters loneliness and stifles love.

Like Romancers, Pleasers want a lot of affection; but whereas Romancers want it all from one person, Pleasers want a little of it from everyone. What their relationships lack in depth, they make up for in sheer numbers. They think that being loved a little by a lot of people translates into being loved a lot. It doesn't.

Pleasers don't focus their attention on any one person, at least not for long. They have mastered the skill of making people feel important and valuable, but they are unable to remain in a deeper relationship long enough to become intimate. They charm people, they tell jokes and are fun to be around, they enjoy helping others enjoy themselves, but they carefully keep people at a distance. They don't know themselves at all well since they're more concerned with activity and work than with reflection, and what they do know of themselves makes them feel uneasy. They have a vague fear of letting people see what's inside.

Most people have at one time or another been drawn to Pleasers. At first it's a wonderful experience to be singled out and made to feel special by someone who is so accomplished and popular. Pleasers often have a good sense of humor and they're able to remember people's names after meeting them for the first time. They're thoughtful and considerate. They go out of their way to be helpful, usually without being asked, and they delight in doing little things that touch people and make them feel appreciated. They like letting others talk about themselves, and people generally would like to get to know them better.

With time, however, people begin to feel disappointed. They thought that something more would come of their friendship with Pleasers, but each time they tried to pursue it, they felt sidetracked. They sense something is missing, although they're not sure what it is. They know they want more substance from Pleasers but find Pleasers seem quite happy with things the way they are. After a while those who have been made to feel special by Pleasers begin to notice and be jealous of the many other people who have also been made to feel special.

Friends who confront Pleasers to tell them of this disappointment usually become even more disappointed. Pleasers want to respond, and they're genuinely concerned when friends feel slighted. That's the bind Pleasers find themselves in. They want to please their friends (and all people are potentially their friends), but some friends will only be satisfied when Pleasers stop trying so hard to be accommodating and simply be who they really are.

Those who try and fail to become more intimate with Pleasers sometimes feel manipulated and angry. Pleasers present a friendly image, one that says they're approachable. And they are approachable—to a point. But once people want to get "too close," they're rebuffed.

When Pleasers lose the approval or appreciation they've come to expect from people, they become angry. They're unaware of being angry and inexperienced at expressing it. Sometimes, when they become angry, they explode in a rage, stepping completely out of character and catching people totally by surprise. Sometimes they deny their anger altogether, but they become cool and distant. They might cover their anger with a humor that isn't really funny or with a polite concern that isn't at all genuine.

Pleasers do fall in love and get married. They're as generous and caring with their spouses and children as they are with their friends. They love and are loved by their families, and they even evoke a sense of admiration from them. They work hard to be good providers. But even in the intimacy of marriage and family life, they're unable to relate with any real depth. Their spouses love and admire them, although they feel they don't get as much time and attention for themselves as they would like. Their children feel the same way. Pleasers don't consciously keep their spouses and children at a distance, just as they don't consciously keep others at a distance. They just don't know how to let others know them or become intimate. Their spouses and children sometimes feel as if they're showpieces, trophies, signs of accomplishment, one more thing Pleasers have done well. If marital problems develop, people are surprised because they think so highly of Pleasers. They assume it must be the other person's fault.

Many people don't try to get any closer to Pleasers. They're content to be friends in a general sort of way. After all, Pleasers are enjoyable to be around, and they don't ask for much in return.

Barbara met the chief administrator of a nearby hospital, and the two of them quickly became friends. Like Barbara, JoAnne was dynamic and vivacious and deeply committed to her work. Since they both served on the board of an accreditation committee, they decided to have lunch together before their monthly meetings. Barbara wanted to become closer friends with JoAnne who seemed quite open to the possibility, but whenever they tried to plan something not connected with work, JoAnne became evasive. She was always too busy with her latest project or with some new program, but she promised Barbara they would get together soon. Barbara once complained to another friend about how she was being treated by JoAnne, and her friend laughed. "You deserve having JoAnne as a friend," the woman said. "The two of you are carbon copies."

Pleasers enjoy working in the helping professions. They like being useful. They're at their best when they work with groups of people and are involved in solving other people's problems.

Pleasers often rise to leadership positions. Although they look confident and self-assured, they sometimes doubt their abilities. But since they need to win approval, they force themselves to take on greater and greater responsibility.

Like Romancers, Pleasers have an insatiable need to be loved. But, unlike Romancers who focus all their needs on one person, Pleasers attempt to have their needs met by being liked and appreciated by everyone. They thrive on attention, and they seek it by being humorous, warm and engaging. Most of all they gain people's attention by making other people feel special. They give to others and they do for others, but they shy away from asking for anything from others. They enjoy entertaining and performing in front of people. They're active people, and they become nervous and ill-at-ease when not engaged in some project. They define themselves much more in terms of what they do—especially what they do for others—than in terms of who they are. They don't know themselves well, and they're generally unaware of their own feelings.

Pleasers find it difficult, if not impossible, to prioritize their relationships. Since they make everyone feel special, they're unable to make just one or two people really special. Their relationships lack depth.

For most of their lives, Pleasers seem to have few problems. They rely on family relationships to meet most of their needs. They derive a great deal of satisfaction from their work or, rather, from people's appreciation of their work.

They seek from others appreciation, not love, and they offer attention, not love. They refuse to risk letting themselves be known well enough to be loved. They give the appearance of loving, but the appearance of love, no matter how convincing, is not the same thing as love. It doesn't fend off loneliness.

In times of crisis, Pleasers become aware of the lack of depth in their relationships and of the loneliness they had previously denied. Their loneliness overwhelms them. No longer able to value the things which had previously satisfied them, they feel overwhelmed by the crisis and plummet into bouts of depression.

Pleasers are like plants with shallow roots. As long as things go well, they thrive and blossom. But as soon as a drought sets in, as soon as their system fails to produce sufficient appreciation and approval, they wither. They lack the deep roots which would have allowed them to endure.

It's a self-perpetuating and self-destructive cycle. Their poor self-image makes them seek approval from others by what they accomplish. Their successes win them the appreciation they want, and performance becomes the measure of their self-worth. They never accomplish enough; one achievement demands another and another. The more they succeed, the more they have to work. They focus on what they do, not on their relationships. They don't notice the lack of intimacy in their lives until things fall apart, and then the depth of their loneliness overwhelms them and reinforces their poor self-image.

The Pleaser's Way out of Loneliness into Love

During our first session together, Barbara sketched out the details of her previous year, beginning with her father's death and the depression which followed. She had spent ten months in a residential mental health program and had worked through much of her depression. She gained insights into the self-destructive elements of her pattern. In the two months since leaving the program, she continued seeing a physician to have her medication monitored. And she asked to see me in order to "get the pieces of her life back together."

"I know," she said, "the things I do that don't work for me. I know I depend on other people's approval too much. I know I work too hard. I know I'm terribly lonely. I know what doesn't work. I don't know what does and I need help finding out."

From Action to Reflection

Pleasers are hard workers. They enjoy what they do, and generally they're successful at what they set out to accomplish. They're dependable; once they set themselves to a task, they complete it. In their work they are gracious and pleasant, concerned about the feelings of their colleagues.

Their gift—commitment to their work—is also the root of their problem. They put too much energy and time into working and not enough into exploring their own inner depths and feelings. Their work, their ceaseless activity, is a defense. It's like a mask that keeps them from knowing who they really are. It also comes between them and the people they relate to.

Pleasers are like stones skipping across the surface of a lake. As long as they're in motion, they stay on the surface of things. They need to slow down so that they can sink into the depths.

For Pleasers to slow down, they must stop. They need to come to a complete and total stop. They've received so much praise over the years for what they do—their jobs, activities, projects, and hobbies—that it's almost impossible for them to stop. And even when they think they're at a standstill, they're probably moving faster than most industrious people.

Once Pleasers begin to slow down, they can begin to reflect. First they'll notice how little depth there is to what they've been doing. They'll see, for example, how they've cared about people without ever knowing them well enough to love them and how they've reacted to problems without thinking them through. Then they'll admit that the praise and appreciation that have kept them going in the past are no longer satisfying. Finally they'll recognize their own needs. They'll see how needing appreciation keeps them from asking for love.

Pleasers need to stop reacting and to start reflecting.

"I can already feel myself getting swept back up in the whirlwind," Barbara observed during one of our early sessions. "I've been out for three months now. And although people are being very good—they tell me to rest and take the time I need—it seems as though they think I should be doing something. And I feel the same way. I think, 'My God, I've been away from work for more than a year now. I've got to get going and make up for lost time.' It's as though I'm on display. I'm trying to convince people I can carry on like I used to.''

"How did you carry on?"

"Oh, you know, by doing, doing, doing. I was always too busy to take care of myself. Keeping busy, in fact, was the thing I knew how to do best.''

"So that's what you want people to expect again?"

"No, not at all. I'm convinced now that that doesn't work for me, but it's so hard to find the middle ground. When I was too sick to work, that was easier. No one expected anything of me. But now that I'm getting better and I'm able to do something, it's hard to keep off that old treadmill.''

"Of course it's hard. But what have you learned lately that can help?''

"Well, I've learned that I've got to take better care of myself. That's what these ten months have taught me.''

"How are you going to do it?"

"I've got to think about other people less and myself more. But I can't tell you how hard that is for me. All my past, all my training, tells me that thinking about myself is selfish and bad.''

"Is it really important that you take care of yourself now?''

"Yes.''

"Then don't tell me how hard it is. Tell me how you're going to do it.''

"It sounds terrible, I know, but I find the best way is for me to ask what *I* need to do. What *I* want to do. What's the best thing for me. Even when I ask those questions, I'm still concerned about others so it's not as if I'm going to turn into this self-centered, egotistical, me-me-me kind of person.''

"Well, what's the best thing for you?"

"For the first time in years, I actually enjoy praying. But I'm not sure I should call it praying. All I do is sit. In the morning I get up and take my time showering and dressing. And then instead of rushing off, I just sit. I've got a comfortable chair. And I look out the window."

"What else?"

"You know something else that's been enjoyable. I'm living in our retirement home—it's a great place to convalesce—and I enjoy visiting with the older sisters. These are women I've known for years. It's funny thinking what I would have done in the past. I'd be the one to organize a program for them. You know, a knitting circle, or a Bingo party, or something. Now I just visit with them. And instead of doing something for them, I listen. It's as if I'm getting to know them for the first time. And you know, they say the same thing about me. They think my time in therapy has made me a new person. I think I've slowed down enough to let them get to know me for the first time. I like that."

From the Many to the Few

Pleasers have a gift for relating to a variety of people. They enjoy large groups, and they ease tension and conflict whenever they exist. People like having Pleasers around. They add a sparkle of life to any gathering.

They're less able, however, to relate to individuals with any real depth. They spread themselves thin, giving bits of themselves to lots of people but never that much of themselves to any one person.

Just as Pleasers need to stop doing so much in order to slow down and reflect, so they must stop trying to do so well with everyone in order to do better with someone. They've mastered the art of making everyone feel special; now they must learn the discipline of making one person more special than the rest.

This is the hardest task for Pleasers but also the most important one: to commit themselves to the people—a few people—who really matter to them. To do this, they must set priorities. They'll be tempted to relate more deeply with everyone, but doing so is just a variation on their pattern. They must learn a painful lesson: to say "yes" to some people requires saying "no" to others.

As they begin to set priorities in their lives, deciding who is and who isn't important, they must reevaluate their relationships with their families.

"I've gotten together with my family for Thanksgiving now as many years as I can remember," Barbara mused one day. "And I've always looked forward to it. But, you know, this year it feels as if I'm going only because I have to."

"Why do you have to?"

"Because they expect me. And they've all been very good to me. Especially during my illness."

"That's fine. But what would you do if you had your druthers? If you weren't concerned about hurting their feelings, what would you want to do this Thanksgiving?"

"Well, I've been spending a lot of time with two younger sisters who are nurses at our home. And we've had wonderful times together. I've enjoyed just sitting and talking with them. When I was in the treatment program, they told me that making that sort of time to be with people would be good for me. But they didn't tell me it would be this much fun. It's as if I've got friends, real friends. They've rented a beach house and they're going away over Thanksgiving weekend. It sounds ideal. They asked me to join them. And if I could, I'd love to."

"So tell me again why you can't."

"Because of my family."

"Let's suppose you did what you wanted to do, for a change. How would you go about telling your family that you can't be with them without hurting them?"

"I think they'd be hurt no matter what I say."

"That's probably true. But by not going aren't you just hurting yourself?"

"I suppose so, but I wouldn't know how to tell them I'm not coming."

"What does 'suppose so' mean? Does that mean you'd be hurt or not?"

"Yes, I guess so."

" 'Guess' doesn't mean much to me. Can you tell me if that's what you really want?"

"Yes, damn it, that's what I want. But I still don't know how I can do it."

"You know your family better than that. Tell me how you can do it—not without hurting them but with hurting them least."

Barbara reflected for a while and we discussed various approaches. She realized that she could do what she wanted to do, even if it meant excluding people she loved in order to be with people she chose to love more.

From Distance to Closeness

Pleasers keep people at a certain distance, close enough so their accomplishments will be noticed but far away enough so their insecurities won't be. They receive a lot of attention, but they risk very little rejection. Their time with people revolves around activities and projects. Pleasers maintain their distance from others in a number of ways, primarily by keeping active and by refusing to set priorities.

Once Pleasers have become more reflective and have made some initial choices, they can take the most important step of breaking out of their loneliness pattern. They can risk.

They can risk making friends instead of merely being friendly. They can risk loving and being loved instead of seeking and receiving approval.

The risk they must take has three stages. First, they must get in touch with their own needs and desires. They have to admit to themselves that they prefer some people to others—"I want to be this person's friend." Then, they have to share their feelings with someone else—"I want to be your friend." Finally, they have to follow through on their choices. Their past ways of spending time with people— usually in a group or as part of a project—simply don't work. There are more satisfying and riskier ways of being with people, and Pleasers have to explore them.

"How was your week at the beach?" I asked Barbara after Thanksgiving.

"It was wonderful."

"What happened?"

"That's the funny part of it. Almost nothing happened. Would you believe we didn't get up until ten or ten thirty, and one day I slept until eleven. We ate when we wanted to. One of the girls loves to cook, and I let her do all the work. At first I felt so guilty. And then I said to myself, 'Now there you go again.' So I stopped all that. Would you believe it? I talked to myself as if I were a kid. I told myself to sit back and enjoy, to let someone do for me rather than do for her. If it sounds easy, it wasn't. The only thing I let myself do was to say, 'Thank you.' I told her how good everything tasted, and she knew I meant it. And I told them both how wonderful it was to be with them."

She paused. "It sounds as if you had a wonderful time."

"I really did. We took two hours to eat dinner every night. Imagine! And every night we opened a bottle of wine. After we finished the dishes, we sat and had coffee in the living room. We listened to the waves in the distance. I can't tell you how wonderful it was. But best of all were the stories we told. We ended up telling stories about ourselves. And I learned so much about them. And hearing them made me feel that it was O.K. for me to tell them about my life, too. And they listened. It was terrific.

"When my family gets together, we also tell stories. We even tell some of the same stories I told last week. But what a difference. This time the stories were so much more personal. This time I felt free to say anything I wanted. I didn't have to keep worrying about what others would think."

"How are you feeling right now?"

"To be honest, so many good things are happening that I can almost say it was worth going through all that I did to get to where I am."

"It sounds as if you're beginning to enjoy your friends and to let them enjoy you."

"That's it. That's what makes it so great."

The
Loser

*L*oser.

It's a degrading name, not one I'd choose to call anyone. But it's the way some people think of themselves. Even "successful" Losers say they've missed out on the important things life has to offer. They feel cheated, as though they've been short-changed. They think others have been given more—more opportunities, more advantages, more skills or personal gifts—and they feel deprived and resentful. Some Losers are openly hostile, at war with the world, while others turn their anger in on themselves, feeling depressed and envious.

The Pattern

Losers lack a sense of self-esteem. They see little of value or worth in themselves or in what they've done, and they assume others judge them in exactly the same way. They don't love themselves and they don't feel capable of being loved. "No one ever really loved me, and no one ever will." Their terrible self-image makes them desperate. They crave the least sign of affection and doggedly pursue anyone who seems to care; at the same time they dismiss whatever love they find, doubting its authenticity.

Although all Losers imagine themselves to be unloved and unlovable, they do so in very different ways.

Howard was an only son. His mother was quiet, always deferring to her husband, a career army officer. They moved frequently, and Howard, a shy person, never made friends. By the time he was sixteen he was overweight and his face was covered with acne. Nothing went well for him at home or in school. His father wanted him to play football, but he failed to make the team; his mother hoped he would be a good student, but at the end of his sophomore year he was placed on academic probation.

When the school counselor met with Howard because of his poor performance, she knew him only by reputation. His teachers described him as sullen and withdrawn, the kind of boy who was the butt of other people's jokes. As she listened to him talk, she detected a recurring theme of resentment and bitterness. "I know my parents are disappointed in me," he said during one of their sessions. "They think I'm a failure, pure and simple, and they're probably right." Then he paused and added, "But they don't realize how much they disappoint me. They're nothing to boast about themselves. They've never given me anything. Nothing." When she called his parents to talk with them, his father refused to meet with her. "What's the use?" he asked over the phone. "It's a waste of time. The kid's just not willing to work." The mother met with her once and insisted that Howard's problems were his own fault.

Howard dropped out of school during his junior year. He left home and wandered about, earning just enough money to survive. Eventually he joined the navy. Although he became a competent corpsman and earned his high school equivalency, he never felt appreciated by those around him. Gaining even more weight and going bald, he wondered how anyone could ever care about him.

After his tour of service ended, Howard moved in with his parents while he looked for an apartment and job. He was hired as a hospital orderly, and the work was so similar to what he had done as a corpsman that he soon found himself bored by the routine. Although patients and nurses appreciated him, he was disappointed in himself. He had hoped to accomplish more with his life by the time he was twenty-seven.

Once he overheard two of his favorite nurses laughing at him behind his back, and he felt betrayed. A short time later, a pastor visiting a patient invited Howard to church.

Howard visited the church and became involved in a Bible study group where he met a woman who enjoyed talking with him. They thought the same way about the Bible and religion, and he took every opportunity to be around her. They volunteered to work on a church project together, and he told her more and more about himself. He felt that she was as interested in him as he was in her, so he started calling her at home. When she didn't seem as warm and caring on the phone, he worried that she really didn't like him. Finally, convincing himself that his suspicions were unfounded, he asked her out for a date. She was polite, telling him how much she treasured him as a brother in the faith, but she made it clear that she had no desire to develop a deeper friendship with him. "I thought she was different," he told himself, "but she's just like everyone else." That was the last time he went to church.

Some Losers are like Howard. They so desperately need to be loved that when they are shown affection, they instinctively move toward it as a moth to light. But equally instinctively they mistrust someone's love for them so they frequently behave in a way that makes their worst predictions come true. Losers demand too much of people who express concern for them or they test them to see if they're sincere, and after a while their demands and tests offend the people who would love them.

Many Losers look at themselves and see only failure. They feel inept around others and ill-at-ease in any relationship. Although they can't remember ever having been loved, they can recall countless examples of being neglected and rejected. They feel pathetic and inadequate.

Jean was the fifth child in a family of seven. Her father worked for the city as a mechanic and her mother was a bus driver. They were immigrants, and Jean was embarrassed by their accent. She was also embarrassed by her clothes, hand-me-downs from her sisters. Although the family was close-knit, Jean was the "odd-person-out." Her parents had an easy way of enjoying their other children, laughing and kidding with them, but whenever Jean was around they looked ill-at-ease. Jean would feel their awkwardness and storm out of the room, sulking for days.

Her parents simply didn't know what to do with her. They knew she was smart and high-strung, and they treated her with kid gloves. Her brothers and sisters thought she was stuck up.

Jean excelled in school and won a full scholarship to a university where she majored in computer programming. She went directly into graduate school and completed a doctorate with little difficulty.

All through school Jean associated with students who were as intelligent as she. She found them stimulating and she enjoyed the verbal jousting they engaged in—the quick put-downs and comebacks. Every so often someone in her group developed a friendship with her, and Jean became warm and funny in a less caustic way. But it never lasted. She became possessive, jealous, and increasingly negative, and the other person would begin avoiding her.

Jean eventually gained a tenured faculty position. Her publications earned her a national reputation, and she traveled extensively as a lecturer. Over the years, as much as she enjoyed her successes, she remained basically dissatisfied with her life. Her biting wit and unpredictable temper kept people at a distance, and she never found the special person she longed for. She became all the more bitter and sarcastic.

Some Losers are more like Jean than like Howard. They have no apparent reason to describe themselves as incompetent or unsuccessful. Often they can point to a skill that sets them apart from others. It takes on enormous importance to them, and they build their lives around it since it's their one hope of gaining respect and affection. But even if they're successful, their self-esteem is undermined by their inability to relate to others in a satisfying way. Clasping all the tighter to their achievements and feeling all the less satisfied by them, these Losers feel out-of-place and vulnerable. They defend themselves by hiding behind a brash and aggressive exterior. The more they call people's attention to their successes and skills, the more they themselves feel their loneliness.

Losers are made from the inside, not from the outside. Others may describe them as successful, talented, and attractive; it makes no difference. Losers see only their own failures, incompetence, and ugliness.

At the heart of the Loser's self-consciousness lies the stinging assessment: "No one has ever really loved me and no one ever will." Although all Losers share the same self-image—unloved and unlovable—no two Losers look alike.

When George first came to see me, he was thirty-eight years old. From the beginning I was impressed by how comfortable he made himself in my office as he talked about himself. He was handsome and articulate, and he radiated a sense of self-confidence. He spoke a lot about being "in control," mostly of his own feelings and life, but I suspected that he needed to be in control of our conversation as well.

George was a social worker. He told me that he was having problems with his co-workers and that his supervisor had suggested he seek help. He came, he said, asking for advice but he sounded more as if he were giving it.

George portrayed himself as the "poor little boy who made good," and he had indeed overcome many painful obstacles. When he was three years old, his father deserted him and his mother, leaving them impoverished. An uncle took them into his home and supported them, but he was an alcoholic, and George and his mother never felt secure.

George excelled at school and put himself through college. He graduated with a major in psychology and landed a job at the university's counseling center. He found little satisfaction in the work—mostly tabulating test scores—and quit after the first year.

Deciding he wanted to be a minister, George entered a

seminary where again he excelled. He worked for a year as a pastoral intern at a large suburban parish, and, at the end of internship, his pastor wrote an evaluation which praised him in all areas except one. He commented favorably on George's sermon preparation and delivery, but he detected a consistent negativity toward the church. He concluded, "He always has an axe to grind." During the year before ordination, the director of pastoral studies asked to speak with him. She told him that the pastor's comments raised questions in her own mind and made her recall times when George had criticized the church. She wondered whether he would be happy as a minister. He reacted angrily, telling her that she was as negative as the pastor, and he questioned whether the church had any room for a prophetic voice. After completing his degree, he decided not to become a minister. "They're all hypocrites anyway," George maintained. "They're no better than anyone else."

George returned to college once again and completed a Master's in social work. His classmates were impressed by his experience and his ability to articulate insights into complex problems, and his professors were equally impressed. They helped him get a job at a substance abuse clinic. The head of the social work department recognized George's gifts and assigned him to lead several therapy groups. After some time of working with him, George's co-therapists were less favorably impressed. They complained about his authoritarian style and arrogance. When his director cited their complaints, she asked George to be more of a team player. "That's easy for her to say," George told me, "but she's not teamed up with a bunch of turkeys."

I summarized what George had said about himself and concluded, "You've told me all about what you've done and about the people you work with. But you haven't talked at all about the other people who are important in your life."

George moved in and out of relationships even more frequently than he changed careers. Women found him attractive, and he went through a succession of brief affairs.

Breaking up was always the woman's fault. The women he met turned out to be too possessive and dependent, not intelligent enough, or only interested in sex. "I've got nothing against women, mind you," he admitted, "but for some reason I end up with the ones who don't know how to handle themselves in a relationship."

When I asked about the men he knew, George said he had lots of friends. "Most of them live in other parts of the country, though, and I don't see them very often," he said. "There was one guy who still lives here in town, but he's not my friend anymore. I felt real close to him once, and I thought we were going to be great friends. And then he put the move on me. You know, he made a pass. I pushed him away, and he had the nerve to tell me I'd been leading him on. The guy's real sick."

After three weeks of listening to George, I began questioning some of the patterns I saw in the incidents he talked about. I pointed out, for instance, how he blamed everyone else for what was wrong in his life. When I wondered about the part he played in all this, he was completely taken aback. "You're just like my supervisor at work," he said, "always making it sound as if something's wrong with me." I wasn't surprised when he failed to show up for our next appointment. And I wouldn't be at all surprised to learn that he's now telling others about a counselor he saw for a time who was more of a problem than a help.

Some Losers, like George, don't look like Losers. They seem to have everything they want, and a lot of things others might envy them for. People are often attracted to this sort of Loser, especially at first, but whenever a misunderstanding or problem occurs, they feel put down, as though whatever went wrong was their fault. Quick to cite their own accomplishments and abilities, they seem supremely self-confident. But they're Losers, nonetheless, and they're the hardest ones to spot. I've learned to recognize this type of Loser only with experience. If they're lonely, it's not their fault. Whenever I work with someone like George, I'm reminded of a line from Shakespeare about the person who "protests too much." Losers say they're good and worthy of being loved. They say they're lonely because others are unloving. And while I know they believe what they're saying, I also suspect that they fear the opposite is true: they fear that they're lonely because they're unlovable. They're so frightened of that possibility that they flatly dismiss anyone who suggests they are in some way responsible for their own loneliness.

Howard, Jean, and George look different, but they're all Losers. In each case one thing remains constant: Losers feel so little self-esteem that they devalue any sense of worth in themselves or what they do. They feel totally incapable of being loved in the way they want.

We all feel inadequate to some degree. We can all point to any number of areas of our lives which cause us shame and guilt. And we can all remember times when our failures and faults overwhelmed us, plunging us into self-pity and helplessness. But Losers are extremists. They tend to discount whatever gifts they possess and dismiss their successes, and they do so because they can only see what they lack. Their faults, defects, and deprivations make them lose all perspective. When I counsel people like this, I tell them to hold their hands up and move them in front of their eyes until they're almost covered. "What do you see?" I ask. Of course, they say, "I can't see anything but my hands." That's precisely what they do with their own inadequacies and failures. They hold their negative self-appraisal so close to their eyes that they lose any sense of proportion. They see only what they don't have and wish they had. When they stop focusing on what causes them pain, it doesn't go away but it does become a much smaller part of a much larger reality.

In spite of their own denials, Losers aren't Losers because of any "objective" deficiency or failure. No one knows from the outside who is or is not a Loser. We've all been amazed and even humbled by people who have everything going against them and yet who appear content with their lives, even happy. I once spoke with a woman who poured out a pathetic story of one loss after another, of hardship and grief, and I found myself thinking, "If ever anyone had a right to give up and wallow in self-pity, this is the person." Fortunately, I kept my thoughts to myself. Without denying her pain and regrets, her outrage and doubt, she made it clear that she wasn't about to give up. And the last thing she wanted from me or from anyone else was pity. It's pointless to judge another person's life on the basis of apparent success or ability. The contentment we seek is rooted in something deeper than achievement and appearance. People make themselves Losers not because of their failures, inadequacies or disabilities—no matter how severe or incapacitating. They make themselves Losers because of their own inner self-perception.

Losers are made from the inside, not from the outside.

There's no denying that other people greatly influence how we feel about ourselves. Some people are continually told, directly and indirectly, that they don't measure up to society's norms of talent, beauty, or worth. But people are Losers because they've made themselves that way in their own eyes. They tend to discount what they have going for them by focusing on what makes their lives painful or incomplete. Being skilled or incompetent, gifted or disadvantaged, respected or ignored, makes little difference. At heart people are Losers because they blind themselves to whatever would make them feel loved and lovable.

Relationship with Parents

Most Losers brood over the past, recalling disappointment and rejection. They talk about the past as though it's as real to them as the present, and they have incredibly sharp memories for the details of long-ago injuries. One man can't even speak of his parents to this day without growing angry.

He describes his father as a tyrannical and overbearing bully. "My mother," he adds "played right along with him. I couldn't do anything right. Whenever I complained about what Dad did, she told me not to pay it any attention, saying, 'You know how your father is.' I don't know what was worse, his abuse or her pretending nothing was wrong."

I asked him if there had been anyone else who had loved him.

"Oh sure," he conceded. "My grandmother. She was always around, looking after me, making me cookies. You know, the typical grandmother sort of thing. She loved me, I suppose, but she had to. She's a grandmother. And that's what grandmothers are supposed to do, love their grandchildren."

If they remember someone who cared about them, inevitably they belittle that love or dismiss it by insisting that the person had to love them for one reason or another.

But some Losers remember the past in a less focused way. They feel bad about what happened, but they can't recall any specific events which caused those feelings. Asked to sum up their childhoods, they respond, "It was okay." One woman grew up in a large Italian family. Both her parents worked to provide a nice home for their children. "My mother and father loved me," she reports. "I never doubted that. Of course, they loved all of us. I was the good little girl, but one of my sisters was retarded and she got most of the attention in my family until she died. I was a senior in high school by then."

Still other Losers can't remember much at all about their earliest years, although they have a clear sense that things didn't go well. One man came to see me after attending a conference on child abuse. He said he had no memories of the first seven years of his life. "I've seen pictures of the house we lived in at the time and I've heard stories about what we did as a family, but I sure can't recall anything on my own. Nothing. It's as if someone pulled a curtain across that part of my brain. Then I was sitting through this work-shop on child abuse. And as I listened, it was as if someone were kicking me in the stomach. Now I'm beginning to wonder. Was I abused? Is that what I'm blocking? I just don't know."

Regardless of how well they remember their past, Losers expend a lot of energy on what happened or didn't happen to them as children. Generally they have a negative attitude toward their parents, an attitude which often becomes obsessive. They think about their parents all the time, and they talk about them to anyone who will listen—sometimes seriously, sometimes in jest, but always casting themselves in the role of victim.

In spite of their harsh appraisal of their parents, Losers keep returning to them in an unconscious effort to win the love they never found in the first place. Losers are bound to their parents, and love isn't always the tie. Sometimes it's resentment; sometimes it's just the never-ending search to find out what went wrong. In the beginning Losers may well have been "victims," but later they victimize themselves by continuing the same self-defeating patterns that were inflicted upon them as children.

All Losers feel deprived and to a greater or lesser degree blame their parents for what they lack. Some believe that their parents didn't love them at all, while others would say they were loved but not as much as someone else. Either way—not loved at all or not loved enough—Losers go through life harboring two fundamental convictions. First, they believe that they lack something essential, a lack that makes them unlovable. Second, they believe that someone else is to blame for their deficiency. The first conviction makes them desperate—they have to acquire whatever it is that will make them lovable. The second conviction makes them angry—they resent others for not giving them what they need or for having more of it than they do.

Relationship to Others

Resentment and blame are the cornerstones upon which Losers build all their later relationships.

When Losers compare themselves to others—which they do constantly—they end up with the short end of the stick. Others are smarter, richer, better looking, luckier, more graceful and sociable; the list of their advantages is endless. And the list of Losers' disadvantages is equally endless. Their lack of self-esteem makes Losers overestimate others and devalue themselves, so their comparisons are generally inaccurate, but that's not all.

Losers think their disadvantages are caused by other people's advantages. It hurts them to think, "I have less than you." But that pain turns into resentment and blame since they believe, "I have less than you because you have more than I."

All Losers are angry. Some turn their anger outward toward others while some turn it in on themselves, but all are angry.

Losers who project their anger outward can be sarcastic and bitter. Their jokes conceal barbs, and when they laugh it's at the expense of others. Even their compliments put people down. At times they let everyone know in no uncertain terms just how angry they are, while at other times they do so in a passive-aggressive way, smiling as they rub salt in people's wounds. They feel as though they've been put down all their lives and think it's only fair to put others down. It's their way of achieving equality. Since they can't imagine building themselves up, they tear other people down. But their strategy doesn't make them feel any better about themselves: others avoid them and they're left all the more lonely and bitter.

Some Losers turn their anger in on themselves. They've been rejected so many times that they internalize all the abuse and blame themselves for their misery. They may not look angry at all. They may look calm and accepting when actually they've merely resigned themselves to their misfortune. They shrug their shoulders as if to say, "What's the use?" Resigned to the fact that they're no good, they keep their anger, resentment, and blame inside where no one else can see it. If it manages to sneak out at all, it looks like depression.

These Losers are so afraid of being put down that they put themselves down before anyone else can do it. They've perfected what I call the "Don't hit me, I'm already down" defense. In order to protect themselves from being criticized in any way, they make people feel sorry for them. They point out all their own deficiencies and failures before anyone else has a chance to. Who would want to criticize people who already feel so bad about themselves?

Anger—whether it's expressed or internalized—controls the lives of Losers.

Losers have problems with people who are in authority over them since they remind them of their parents who were never satisfied. They may openly distrust authority figures, questioning their motives and competence, opposing them at every turn. Then they look a lot like angry little kids throwing a temper tantrum. Or they may be cooperative and helpful, seeking the approval of those in authority. They would never consider standing up to their bosses or opposing them in any way. When they disagree or feel unappreciated, they'll do anything—get sick, change jobs, move— to avoid the conflict they fear.

Out of Loneliness into Love

Losers have many gifts, although they themselves don't recognize them. They are introspective and reflective. They're able to admit their own shortcomings and failings. They know both their pain and their desire for intimate relationships.

As with all the patterns of loneliness, their strengths are

also their undoing. They need to be balanced by other strengths, ones they haven't developed.

It is difficult for Losers to break out of their loneliness—and Losers themselves are the first to protest how difficult it is—but it can be done. Losers have faced so much adversity in their lives that they have a great deal of inner strength. They typically use their strength against themselves by being stubborn or resistant, but strength is strength and it can be used effectively to help them tear down the prison walls of their confinement.

From Self to Other

Losers tend to be incredibly self-centered. They act as though the whole world is no larger than the circle of their own lives. They ask only one question in their evaluation of anything: "How does this affect me?" Their self-centeredness shows up most noticeably in the way they talk. No matter how the conversation starts or what the topic is, Losers inevitably end up talking about themselves. Some talk about how bad they are and how they've always failed at whatever they've tried. Others talk about all they've done and how others have praised them for their accomplishments. The two approaches may look different, but they're actually identical: Losers talk about themselves.

Sometimes I can recognize Losers just by the way they deal with me. Even on the first appointment, they plunk themselves down in a chair, hardly bothering to acknowledge me, and begin talking about themselves and their problems. After a few meetings, I point this out to them. From then on they try to pay more attention to me, but they're so awkward that it's funny. When we can both laugh about it, things begin to change. Gradually what began with such contrived effort—paying attention to me—becomes more natural, and eventually they genuinely want to know how I'm doing.

Losers have to start thinking and talking about others.

They can begin by noticing other people. Having fixed their eyes on themselves and their own inadequacies, they need to turn their gaze elsewhere. They need to look at other people and see them as they are, showing concern by listening to them and remembering what's important to them. Since their lives have revolved around their own concerns and their need to protect themselves from abuse and rejection, Losers will initially be awkward in expressing their concern for others. Still, it requires practice. I often remind them of an early VW "bug" advertisement. It showed only the VW symbol and a stick shift with the words, "After a while, it becomes automatic."

From Negative to Positive

My mother always used to say, "There's a little bad in the best of us and a little good in the worst of us." Losers acknowledge the bad that's in the best of us, and they do so with a vengeance. But they don't see the good that's in the worst of us, not in others and especially not in themselves. Actually, they may acknowledge the good in others, but they see it as something that makes them bad. They have great difficulty seeing the good in themselves, and even when it's brought to their attention they discount it.

They need to recognize the good in themselves and to value it, to say, "These are some of the things I've accomplished, these are some of my skills, these are some of my strengths, and I'm proud of them." Likewise, they have to realize that other people's gifts don't deprive them of anything at all. Other people's riches don't impoverish them.

After seeing Beth for six months, I thought we were making little progress. We kept covering the same territory. The problems were always different, but she always talked the same way. She spent every session recounting the massive hemorrhage of bad events of the previous week. The events changed, but not the attitude. Whenever I made any positive comment, she seemed not to hear me. Once I complimented her on her dress, and she said, "To tell you the truth, I hate this dress. I bought it on sale." As time went on, I found myself dreading our time together. Finally I decided to tell her how I was feeling about our meetings.

"Beth, let me tell you something I've noticed. In each of our sessions, there's a similarity. Each time you sit in that chair, you talk about only things that have gone wrong."

"That's the trouble with you counselors. You're always finding fault."

"Beth, you just did it again."

She lapsed into silence, looked hurt and rejected.

"Beth, let me start over. As I have come to know you better, I've seen some things about you that are admirable and likeable. But each time I mention them or say anything positive about you, you pay me no attention. You go right back to grumbling about something."

"So what am I supposed to do about it?"

"Why don't you tell me what you think would help."

"Well, obviously you think I should be talking about positive things."

"I think that what you're doing keeps you depressed. And in fact it depresses me too. I'd like you to try something new. For our next two sessions, I don't want to hear one thing that's gone wrong. All you can talk about are the good things that have happened to you."

She left the session pouting, and I wondered whether she would return the next week. She did return, and she talked about the events that had gone well for her since our last meeting.

"I made a list," she said, "so I wouldn't forget anything."

At first she looked as though she were taking medicine, but she continued the exercise for the next several weeks. I saw parts of her I hadn't seen before, attractive things. Before I had complimented her on exterior things, like her dress. Now I began noticing her inner beauty. When she talked about her problems, she spoke with less bitterness and more hope.

"You know," she commented one day, "I hate to admit it. But I can tell a difference. When I talk about the good things that happen, I feel better about myself."

Although she still tended to lapse into negativity, she did so less regularly, and even then she wasn't as negative as she had previously been. She even began laughing. When I commented on how much I liked her new look (she had lost weight), she simply smiled and said, "Thank you."

From Blaming to Accepting

Blaming helps Losers deny their pain. If they assumed responsibility for all the negativity they feel, Losers would be overwhelmed. Blaming perpetuates their negativity while shifting the focus; they put the responsibility on others, especially on their parents. As they become more positive about themselves, Losers have less need to project their negativity onto others. Whenever anything goes wrong, Losers automatically slip into their old pattern of looking for someone to blame. They have to learn to accept responsibility for their own lives, their mistakes as well as their achievements.

I had been seeing Jackie for almost a year. During one session, she reported: "During my coffee break, Sherlie—she's the woman who's sort of my boss—said, 'Did you have car problems this morning?' I never liked the woman anyway. She's always criticizing me. Always finding fault. There's nothing I can do to please her."

"Back up a minute," I interrupted. "You lost me. What did she say to you?"

"She asked me about my car. But I know she was putting me down for coming in late. My daughter was in one of her usual bad moods, and by the time I got her off to school, I was behind schedule. I was fifteen minutes late. But it wasn't my fault. My daughter's been causing me more and more problems lately.''

"I'm not sure that's what your boss was really getting at," I said. "But let's suppose for a moment that you're right. Maybe she was criticizing you for coming in late. So? What's so bad about that?''

"I didn't say it was so bad.''

"But you did. Look at all the trouble you went to making your daughter responsible. If you really believed it wasn't that bad, why go to that much bother?''

As soon as Losers take responsibility for something that's gone wrong in their lives, they find much to their surprise that they aren't devastated. They can say, "I made a mistake," or "I was wrong," without having to think, "I'm a bad person," or "No wonder no one loves me."

The
Loner

*L*oners are the classic "strong and silent type." They look imperturbable, as though nothing affects them, and they rarely show any feelings. Others see them as calm, steady, reliable, reserved, aloof. But even when they appear distant and unconcerned about the swirl of events and emotions all around them, Loners have a certain appeal. Similar to the way cowboys are portrayed in movies, Loners stay calm under pressure, face adversity without flinching, and after they have won the day ride off—alone—into the sunset.

A Loner

A high school counselor called, asking me to work with a senior at her school. "Joe used to be a model student," she reported, "good grades, first-string on the football team, respected by his teachers and liked by his peers. But a few months ago, his English teacher told me she was worried about him. His work had deteriorated and he was even more withdrawn than usual. I didn't think much about it, frankly, until his coach said almost the same thing. I spoke with Joe two or three times, but without much success. I knew his grandfather had died and I suspect that has something to do with it, but he assured me he'd be O.K."

She paused. "I've kept an eye on his performance since then, and now I'm even more worried. He's still doing poorly in class and he may be cut from the team. He isn't talking to anyone. I called his parents and his mother said they'd noticed a change in him too, but they weren't concerned. She said he acted like this years ago when his brother died and he got through that crisis after a while. She and her husband tended to let him work through his problems on his own. Part of me agrees with his mother—I think he'll be all right in the long run—but part of me continues to worry. Maybe I'm overreacting, but last year another student went through much the same thing and she killed herself. I don't want to take any chances. What do you think?"

It's never fair to judge someone based on another person's reports, but the school counselor described someone I would call a Loner.

When Joe first came to see me, we introduced ourselves and exchanged a few pleasantries. Then he sat in his chair and waited for me to do something. He was a pleasant looking young man, athletically-built and soft-spoken.

Normally I begin a counseling relationship by asking "Why are you interested in counseling at this time?" but experience has taught me that a person referred to me by someone else usually says something like: "Because I was sent" or "Because my teacher told me I should." Although Joe appeared at ease, simply sitting still, I imagined that he was probably feeling threatened and hesitant to talk. I began the conversation by reporting what his counselor had told me and concluded, "It seems you're experiencing some difficulties. I can appreciate how hard it is to talk to someone you don't know."

He remained silent for a while, shook his head, and said, "I think people are making too much of all of this."

"That's very possible," I said, "but why don't you tell me your side of the story?"

"I'm having some trouble with classes, and I've lost interest in football. That's all."

"But why?"

"What do you mean?"

"Well, I'm wondering why all this is happening at this particular time."

"My parents think it's because of my grandfather's death."

"And what do you think?"

"I don't know."

"Were you close to your grandfather?"

There was another long pause. Looking off into the distance and, haltingly at first, he began talking about his grandfather. I encouraged him to continue. As he went on, he grew more relaxed in the conversation, but I noticed how his eyes made little contact with mine. In fact even when he faced me directly, he looked at a picture above my desk. Joe spoke about his grandfather in a way that clearly showed he loved him, although he never spoke directly about his feelings.

When I commented that his grandfather must be very special to him, Joe withdrew. "I guess he was," he said. It was easy to feel his awkwardness.

When I asked Joe about his lack of interest in school and football, he admitted he felt tense and unsettled. And again he ended the conversation. At the close of our first hour, I asked him what he made of our time together.

"It was O.K."

"Would you like to get together again?"

"I guess so."

Normally I wouldn't settle for such a non-committal response, but I realized that "I guess so" was the most I could hope for from Joe. I asked what his schedule looked like, making him take some responsibility for setting up our next meeting. He gave no sign of leaving until I stood up and said I'd be glad to see him next week.

Loners don't give much of themselves. They make other people do much of the work in a relationship and most of the work in a conversation.

Joe came regularly, always on time, never missing an appointment. With time he renewed his interest in school and football. Still he shied away from talking to me about what his grandfather's death meant to him. He answered my questions clearly, but I never felt that he trusted me enough to be open and relaxed in talking about himself. He enjoyed the attention I gave him and said that our sessions were helpful, but I had the vague sense that he was using me. I was a problem-solver, not a person.

One time I asked him what he thought about me personally, and he said he found our time "very useful."

"I'm glad it's been beneficial, but what do you think of me as a person."

"I think you're a nice guy."

"What else do you feel about me?"

He shifted in his chair and responded, "I just told you. I like talking to you, and I think you're a nice guy."

Loners can't talk about their feelings with any ease or comfort, and they're almost totally incapable of telling others how they feel about them.

Over a period of time, Joe told me about his childhood and his family. He was fifteen months younger than his brother, Matt, who was by contrast out-going and active. Matt gathered the neighborhood children and organized their games and expeditions. He had an infectious sense of humor and a ready ability to relate to adults as well as to his contemporaries. Matt and Joe liked each other, feeling that they were friends as well as brothers. Matt naturally included Joe in all his activities, and Matt's friends became Joe's.

Joe knew instinctively that his mother had a special affection for Matt. They were alike in their liveliness, quick wit, and ease at relating with others. Joe was more like his father, a man whose friendly reserve and shyness kept him from expressing warmth and closeness. His family realized what his friends only sensed: although Joe was present and could always be counted upon, he was also detached and remote. He liked spending time by himself.

Matt died of leukemia when Joe was thirteen years old. Joe was devastated. He had always counted on Matt, and now he had no one to turn to. At the funeral his mother wept and Joe tried putting his arm around her as he had often seen Matt do, but he felt awkward and she pulled away.

Joe felt as though he were going to explode with all the feelings he had inside, and he wanted to talk to someone. But Matt was the one he would have talked to, and Matt was gone. He had lost his brother and only friend, but he lost even more. Matt had allowed him to engage others and be active, and suddenly Joe lost those opportunities. He felt more alone than ever. Like his father, Joe didn't cry at the funeral.

I could tell that Joe had a lot of mixed feelings connected with his brother's death, feelings he had never talked about, feelings that terrified him and made him withdraw into himself.

Feelings of any sort, but especially feelings like anger or guilt, confuse Loners and cause them to retreat into themselves. It's as though they have to sort things out and clean them up before they can talk to anyone else.

Joe's life settled down more. He graduated from high school and entered community college. We continued to meet regularly, and I continued to press him to talk about how things in his life affected him emotionally. It was slow going. Joe talked about problems or what he was doing. To his irritation, I kept asking him, "How are you feeling right now?" He was hesitant to talk about his feelings and even more reluctant to talk about how he felt about me. Although he learned to share his emotions, he remained cautious about doing so.

Toward the end of his second year at the community college, Joe explored his options for the next year. Although he clearly wanted to attend the university and was quite capable of doing so, he postponed making any decisions. I asked him why he was procrastinating. Reluctantly, he admitted he enjoyed our time together, and he didn't like the thought of moving out of town.

"I think I'll miss you," he said.

I was surprised. It was the first time Joe had expressed—even indirectly—personal regard for me. I assured him of my care for him and of my desire to meet with him whenever he returned to visit.

During our next session Joe clearly had something on his mind. "I know we don't have many more sessions together," he started, "but I want to talk about sex." Even raising the topic made him feel awkward. He had had little sexual experience, he said, and this in itself bothered him. Growing up, he felt more comfortable relating to boys and he rarely dated. He recalled having some sexual fantasies in his early teens that made him wonder whether he was homosexual. This fear increased his tendency to pull back into himself, and his unwillingness to talk about it made it all the worse. Joe described his fears and concerns with remarkable openness and honesty. He was eager to talk and we spent three sessions discussing what had been carefully hidden for so many years. In time, Joe realized there was nothing in his experience or feelings to indicate that his basic orientation was homosexual. He also came to see how he had let his fear of talking about his feelings imprison him. Later, as he thanked me he told me how much he valued our relationship and how much I meant to him. His words were spoken with warmth and affection.

I saw Joe from time to time, usually during school breaks when he returned to visit his parents. At the end of his junior year, he told me of his plans to work with a volunteer program in Appalachia, and, almost in passing, he mentioned a woman he was dating. He made the football team and was elected co-captain. During his senior year, he became "serious" with a woman, and he talked about marrying her as soon as they both established themselves in their professions. Sensing that this was one of our last times together, I asked him to review how he had seen himself develop.

"I'm almost embarrassed to remember our first meeting. I sure didn't realize it at the time, but I was so isolated and out of touch with my feelings. I know I still tend to shut down whenever I'm overwhelmed by what's happening around me. And I know that's always going to be a part of me, but relating to you and now to Diane has made me confident that I can love someone and allow myself to be loved."

The Loner Dynamic

To others, Loners appear integrated, calm, and self-assured. But Loners don't feel that way at all. They are afraid. They're frightened of the inner turmoil they feel, of being overwhelmed by emotions they don't understand and can't control. They're always on guard, terrified that the mess that's inside will somehow leak out, convinced that others would reject them if they saw it. They need to be in control of themselves at all times, and they avoid spontaneity. Loners say, in effect, "Leave me alone until I get myself together. Then, when I'm presentable, I'll let you know me."

Fear makes Loners keep people at a distance, and in turn loneliness contributes to their fear. And the cycle begins again. Their exaggerated fear drives them deeper into isolation which only intensifies their need of intimacy.

More clearly than Romancers, Pleasers and Losers, Loners make themselves lonely by refusing to engage in relationships. Like Romancers, Loners long for someone who will love them and take away their loneliness, but they are passive and make no effort to seek such a person. Like Pleasers, Loners care about what others think of them, but they're content as long as others don't judge them negatively. And like Losers, Loners are passive, but they aren't angry or resentful.

The word I think of to describe Loners is "flat." It's hard to get a rise out of them, and it's unlikely to see them in the depths of despair. They may be pleased, but rarely overjoyed; irritated, but seldom outraged. Even the way they speak—their voice—is carefully modulated.

Loners are passive, frequently withdrawn, and difficult to engage in conversation. They wait for others to take the initiative, and they make better listeners than responders, better observers than participants. Since they avoid taking risks, they rarely make mistakes or look foolish. They appear to be well-integrated, as though they have no needs, no rough edges, no insecurities. They are often pleasant, bright, capable, reliable, and respected. People depend on them without expecting much from them in terms of emotional support.

Their pattern of avoiding deep relationship reaches all the way back into their childhood. Their families may have been affectionate and close-knit or cold and unresponsive; it makes no difference. For some reason, they were always considered "different." They may have been loved and appreciated, even admired, but others in their family knew there was something unusual about them. They were ever so slightly removed from the emotional hub of the family. They were self-sufficient. They may have been less active than their siblings, and they were certainly more content to play by themselves. They weren't as warm and affectionate as other children their age; they didn't go running to their parents to give them hugs and they were shy around strangers. They seemed mature for their age, and people thought of them as little adults. They rarely asked for attention. They enjoyed being praised for their accomplishments, but they didn't know how to respond to any direct display of affection.

Loners shut down emotionally. They share information. They talk about things that interest them or about people they care for, but they don't talk about how they feel. And even if they do talk about their feelings, they do so in a guarded way that doesn't let their feelings show. Self-conscious when others pay too much attention to them, they dislike being the center of attention. They prefer standing one step removed from the group and watching how other people act.

Loners work their problems out by themselves. They gather information—like a squirrel collecting nuts—and they process it when they're alone. When they've considered everything to their satisfaction and they're confident they've made no mistake, they present the finished product to others.

Loners play emotional hide-and-seek. They show just enough of their sensitivity so that others are attracted to them, but they conceal enough so that others are left wanting more. Loners enjoy having others want to know more about them; being pursued by others isn't the same thing as intimacy, but it gives Loners a taste of intimacy while leaving them protected.

Like Joe, many Loners are pleasant and attractive. People want to know them. At the same time talking to Loners can be difficult, since they do little to keep the conversation alive and moving. They avoid committing themselves by saying "I don't know" or "I guess" and by answering a question with a question. When pressed, they may respond honestly but they're always careful not to divulge too much about themselves.

Loners connect with others in a surface way. Their fear of letting themselves be known makes them shy away from making any personal commitments. They don't want to be alone. They like being around others. But they avoid entering too deeply into relationships. They set limits: "Come this far and no farther."

Their fear makes them relate to people they judge to be safe: adults, mentors, peers who ask for little and make no demands. They are most comfortable while relating to people around a problem or a project. They work well in group settings that are structured, such as teaching, although on the whole they lack the interpersonal skills required by less formal situations. They are drawn to helping professions, such as ministry, because they are gentle, patient, and accepting of others. Their inability to be assertive or to take risks, however, hampers their effectiveness in whatever they do. They are often at a loss for words, and they can be exceptionally stubborn. They put distance between themselves and others, and when people leave them alone, they feel relieved.

Loners haven't learned the language of relationships. Everyone finds it difficult to express feelings, especially affection, but while others are willing to risk—to stumble around and make mistakes in an effort to learn—Loners are not. They don't allow themselves to make mistakes, to look foolish or incompetent. If they can't say exactly the right thing in precisely the right way, then they won't say anything at all.

Loners have learned to be content by themselves. Whenever they're threatened by a problem they can't solve or by strong feelings or by a situation which may expose them, they retreat into themselves. They may physically withdraw, simply leaving the place where the tension exists, or they may run away emotionally. It's as though they're there, but not there. Distance, withdrawal, passivity, and silence are all ways Loners use to avoid committing themselves emotionally.

Few people find it easy to talk about their sexuality, but Loners find it almost impossible. Strong sexual drives, especially during adolescence, overwhelm Loners and drive them all the more deeply into their well-established pattern of withdrawal. Hiding intensifies the fear and gives them all the more reason to keep to themselves. Other people, too, are afraid of their developing sexuality and are confused by it, but Loners add to their fear and confusion by keeping it all within themselves. Without any close friendships, Loners have no one to talk to about their feelings.

Afraid of their sexuality, Loners feel threatened by physical closeness of any sort. It's not that they don't want to be touched and held; it's just that they're afraid of what might happen if they are. Most Loners feel intensely on the inside but their appearance gives no hint of this. People see Loners as cool and detached, lacking in passion, and sense the Loner's unspoken message, "Stay away; don't come too close." They wonder if Loners are different from everyone else; they wonder if Loners have any need for intimacy or touch. They don't realize that they're perceiving not a lack of desire but a product of fear. Loners know their own need for closeness, but, paralyzed by fear and inexperience, they deny their need rather than acknowledge their feelings. In their fantasies, Loners long for someone who will break through their defenses and hold them close.

The Loner's Way out of Loneliness into Love

Loners tend to be attractive people, dependable, reliable and steady. Their silence and willingness to listen allows people to share their feelings, and they are generally helpful. They are reflective and non-judgmental.

Loners have much to offer. They're like hidden treasure. Their way out of loneliness begins when they choose to open themselves up and to allow others to see what's within.

From Caution to Risk

By nature Loners are cautious people.

If they were to go swimming in a strange place, they would carefully approach the water and slowly dip a toe in to feel the temperature. They would never consider diving into the water without first checking for any dangers. Obviously, there's good reason for caution. People are hurt all the time because they jump into unknown depths without first checking for hazards. But Loners carry caution to an extreme. Even if they see others diving into the very same place, they hesitate. They're so careful that the last thing they have to worry about is being foolhardy.

Loners need to jump into relationships, to dive into the murky waters of intimacy and take risks. They can throw caution to the wind because their natural reserve will automatically guard them against inappropriately disclosing themselves to others.

Loners break through their pattern of loneliness by talking about themselves, by saying what they think even when their opinions are only half-formed and open to dispute, even when they aren't sure whether others are really interested in listening. They need to make themselves vulnerable in spite of their awkwardness and fear of being judged. When they want to fade into the background or avoid a challenging situation, they need to plant their feet firmly and refuse to run away. They must learn to value trust and openness more than independence and self-reliance. They must risk appearing foolish, incomplete, or imperfect. They must put themselves on the line and be willing to say, "This is who I am. Take me or leave me."

From Passivity to Activity

Loners use passivity as a defense. It's a way of being cautious. It keeps people at a distance, giving Loners time to sort out their feelings and their responses.

The main way Loners can take risks is by being active instead of passive. They may want initially to try out their new behavior in a "safe" relationship (as with a counselor), but eventually they will have to take risks with others too. Loners tend to approach their problems in relating (as they approach all their problems) by first analyzing them. They have a gift for thinking things through and considering a variety of alternatives. But analysis is simply another form of passivity unless it's put into action. Loners learn new behavior by moving from thinking to feeling and finally to doing. It's not enough for them to say, "I see what I'm doing wrong," or even to desire to do something different; they will learn how to love only by acting. Since they are experimenting with a whole new range of relating, they must expect to make mistakes and to fail. But they can't allow failure to overwhelm them or to justify their not trying again.

Loners leave behind their old habits when they begin to speak up rather than first listen, when they act rather than merely reflect, when they reach out rather than retreat, when they choose to be with others rather than stay alone, when they stop gathering information and begin acting on the data they already have.

From Hiding to Disclosing

Loners move from loneliness into love when they move from solving problems by themselves to working them through with others, when they stop saying, "Leave me alone until I figure this out," and begin saying, "Can you help me? I don't understand this," when they disclose not only their thoughts but also their feelings, and when they no longer allow their sexuality—despite its fear and confusion—to keep them from sharing their feelings.

When Loners let others see them as they are, when they show their anger and disagreement as well as their affection and warmth, when they express their interest in other people and risk getting closer, then they will have moved away from the loneliness of hiding and be well on their way to self-disclosure and love.

The
Repertoire
of
Love

*W*henever I talk to people about how I see them relating to others and to me, I add the proviso, "Now what I've sketched out is a rough draft. I'm painting in broad strokes, and I know the picture needs to be given the finer texture and depth of nuances and qualifications and exceptions. But I'm purposely using primary colors to call your attention to something you might otherwise overlook."

Throughout this book I've been describing patterns of loneliness, patterns which have become so ingrained through years of repetition that they feel natural. They become part of us—like long-standing habits or deeply-held and unquestioned convictions—but they aren't the whole of us. Although I've given the patterns names—Romancer, Pleaser, Loser, and Loner—and called particular people by those names, I don't mean to suggest that we *are* one thing or another. We can't be categorized. Each one of us is unique. And although we may share common patterns of relating, there's no such thing as a Romancer or a Pleaser or a Loser or a Loner. The four patterns of loneliness are categories not of people but of behavior. It would be more accurate to say that we adopt the relational patterns of a Romancer or a Pleaser or a Loser or a Loner. It would be even more accurate to say that at different times and under different circumstances we adopt various aspects of all the patterns. In most of us, though, one pattern predominates and at times it becomes an extreme.

When I wrote about Martin in the fifth chapter, calling him a Romancer, I did so for the sake of clarity and not without reservation. It was easier to say that he was a Romancer than to say that he adopted the pattern of the Romancer. In truth, no one of us is a Romancer, even though we may spend all our lives looking for one person to love and even though we may do all the other things I've said a Romancer does.

It seems like a small point to say that we *act* in a certain way, not that we *are* a certain thing, but it's a crucial distinction. If we are something—a Pleaser, for example—then there's not much we can do. Changing the isolating patterns we've developed over the years is hard work and not without its setbacks and failures, and we're always tempted to give up trying. To throw our hands up in defeat and say, "What's the use? I am what I am and that's it. I can't do anything about it. You can't expect a leopard to change its spots," is an excuse, a reason to stop trying. When people in counseling tell me something to that effect, I refuse to believe them. I respond, "You've related one way most of your life but that doesn't mean you can't do anything about it. To say 'I can't' means 'I won't' or 'I don't want to.' "

We can make the necessary changes in our lives if we acknowledge first that we are who we are largely because of what we do and, second, that we can change what we do. Patterns of loneliness are ways of relating, and although it takes effort and practice and patience, we can change them if we decide that we really want to.

When we first begin changing how we relate to others—especially if we have adopted a particular pattern in an extreme way—we tend to develop equally unsuccessful ways of doing so. We often switch from one extreme to another. If we've consistently sought one other person who would take away all our emptiness (as Romancers do), we may decide to withdraw completely and rely only on ourselves (as Loners do). While we may think we've made a radical change, the reverse side of a problem is still a problem. We've simply learned another way of making ourselves lonely.

As I have described them, the patterns of loneliness are extremes. That's their problem. We isolate ourselves by developing one dominant way of relating and relying almost exclusively on it. It's not at all unhealthy, for example, to say, "I want other people to appreciate me," but it becomes self-defeating when we actually mean, "I need everyone to appreciate me—and that's all I want." To exchange one extreme for another is not the way out of loneliness, although it may be a necessary first step. In what follows I will trace the tendency to move from one extreme to another, the reasons we do so and the problems that result. I will then show how avoiding extremes and tapping the strengths of each particular pattern can help us move out of loneliness into love.

From Romancer to Loner

Toni had been seeing me for a little over a year, and it was clear to both of us that her main pattern was that of the Romancer. She was currently involved with a man she met at work, a man who was "everything I've always wanted—smart, handsome, successful, and single." One day she walked into my office, and I immediately sensed that something was wrong. She slumped into her chair and released a deep sigh.

"Do you know what that man did to me?" she asked, obviously not looking for a response. "He got a promotion and he's moving halfway across country. And to top it off when he tells me about it, he expects me to be delighted. Delighted!"

She took a breath and began again. "All this time I've been thinking he's going to ask me to marry him and he's been thinking about Des Moines. 'We'll stay in touch,' he says to me."

She continued expressing her anger and hurt, and finally concluded, "If I were a Catholic, I'd become a cloistered nun. I don't want to see another man in my whole life. Never! They're all the same. You can't trust any of them."

We sat in silence for a while and then I said, "Toni, I'm

really very sorry this happened and I can appreciate how hurt you are." After a few more minutes of silence, I continued, "But let me tell you what happened to me while I was listening to you. Part of me understood why you were saying what you did. You've been very, very hurt. But part of me felt put down and wanted to say, 'What did I do to deserve this?'"

"What did you do to deserve this?" she snorted. "What's this got to do with you?"

"What's this got to do with me? You just threw me out of your life. You told me I'm not trustworthy."

"I didn't say that."

"But you did. Because you found one man untrustworthy, you've decided no man can be trusted."

"Well, that isn't what I meant."

"I know that isn't what you meant, but I want you to hear what happens when you get upset. When things fall apart, you go right back to your absolutes. You flip from one extreme to another."

"What do you mean?"

"We've looked at the way you tend to fixate on one person—like Ralph—and make the sun rise and set on him. But as soon as something goes wrong, you don't want anything to do with him or with any other man for that matter."

Over the next few sessions Toni reflected on how she had reacted first to Ralph and then to me. "I think I see now," she admitted. "At first I made him everything and then as a result of one conversation I dismissed him completely. At first I trusted one person absolutely and then I trusted absolutely no one. All or nothing—I can see what you mean by extremes."

Romancers set their sights so high that they're bound to fail. They inevitably miss the mark. They long for an all-embracing love so much that when they think they've found the right person they expect perfection. As soon as something goes wrong, and it always does, they throw the person out with the fault and lose everything. Since they do everything with passion, when they lose they lose with passion. They don't fall gently; they hit the earth with a thud.

At first Romancers who have "loved and lost" look a lot like Losers; they hurt and feel sorry for themselves and blame others. But Romancers can't think of themselves as Losers for long. They've been loved too many times before to imagine that they're incapable of being loved again. They're not unlovable, just tired—tired of investing all their time and energy in another person—and they want to rest.

The reaction of Romancers to the pain of losing in love—"Leave me alone"—is the statement of a Loner. They curl up into a ball and withdraw from others in order to recuperate. They may say they're never going to love again (the typical statement of an extremist) but they're merely resting. It's as though they've had the wind knocked out of them and they have to catch their breath before beginning again.

Instead of reacting to their loneliness by withdrawing from others into themselves (as Loners do), Romancers need always to seek the middle ground in relationships. They need to settle for something between "all or nothing."

I was middle ground for Toni. I wasn't capable of satisfying all her needs for care and attention, but I did care for her and give her attention. Although I wasn't the center of her life, I could still be a stable friend she could rely on. In spite of her initial urge never to trust another man, she did continue to trust me. She monitored her tendency to expect everything from one person and eventually worked through her relationship with Ralph. "All right," she admitted, "I still have fantasies about marrying him. But I'm not going to let those fantasies keep me from enjoying what we have. He's a good friend. And I like that."

From Pleaser to Loser

Pleasers want everyone to affirm them at all times. They work hard to win the approval of others, and they go out of their way to avoid being criticized. While society tends to value the ideal of love held by Romancers, it tends to reward Pleasers. They work hard, they're considerate, accommodating, and successful, and they receive a lot of praise and attention for their efforts. The rewards—approval, promotions, raises—keep Pleasers working and achieving and out of touch with their own deeper needs and feelings. Without warning, they may be hit from their blind side. Something goes wrong—Pleasers aren't introspective enough to see it coming—and everything falls apart. They are plunged into a crisis. Everything they've ever valued or worked for or invested in suddenly appears worthless. Their entire lives have revolved around success, and so when failure strikes they don't know what to do about it.

When Pleasers hit rock bottom, they lose all their self-confidence and begin to act like Losers. Since they've invested most of their energy into work and attempted to please a large number of people, when their work fails them they can find no special person to turn to. They say with the Loser, "I've never really been loved and I never will be."

They flip from one extreme—"Everyone cares about me"—to another—"No one loves me."

That's what happened to Sister Barbara, the nun who ran a hospital, presided over her religious community, and suffered a breakdown. She seemed to have many friends, but in facing the crisis of her father's death, she realized how empty her life really was. Before, her work meant everything. Suddenly, it meant nothing. Her world fell apart.

Pleasers have to rebuild their lives, as Barbara did, by setting priorities. They can't be all things to all people, but they can choose to make certain people more special than others. They have to say what's hardest for them to admit, "I love some people more than I love others and I want them to love me." They need to avoid the extreme reaction of the Loser—"I can't please anyone and I'm not going to try"—and decide instead which people they want to please.

From Loser to Romancer

Losers convince themselves that no one can possibly love them. They tend to see only what hurts in their lives, their failures and inadequacies, and to discard their successes and talents. Giving up any hope of ever being loved, they escape into fantasy. That's what makes them like Romancers: their fantasies. Romancers believe that there's one other person in this world who will love and protect them, who will give them undying care and attention. And that's a fantasy. Despairing that they could ever be loved, Losers hope for a miracle, a miracle that looks remarkably similar to the fantasy of the Romancer. In their imagination Losers long for someone special, someone who will do the impossible—love them.

Tim walked into my office, smiling as I'd never seen him do.

"I'm in love. I know you won't believe it. I can't believe it either. And she loves me. It's terrific."

"When we were together just three weeks ago, you didn't say a word about this. What happened?"

"It's the girl at work, Debbie. She sits two desks down from me. She's been working there for a little over a year now and we've never connected, although I can't say I haven't wanted to. Just after you and I met last time, she came up to where I was eating lunch and asked if she could share the table with me. We started talking and we kept talking. She's like me in a lot of ways, shy and not very comfortable around people. But we sure didn't have trouble talking that day. When I went back to work, I couldn't get her out of my mind. And you know what's really amazing? She's not only a lovely person, she's also good looking."

He paused.

"We've been eating lunch together every day since then. It's great. You know, she's always wanted to get to know me just as I've wanted to meet her. I can't believe I'm so lucky. She's what I've been hoping for." He paused again, looked worried, and asked, "What do you say?"

"I say, alleluia. It's great to hear you excited about someone and I'm delighted you feel so special. That's wonderful and I'm happy for you. But I must confess I'm also a bit uneasy. I'm concerned that you might be setting yourself up for a fall."

"You mean you think she's just stringing me along."

"That's not what I mean. I have no idea what she's feeling or thinking, but I do know that you tend to set yourself up for rejection. Love is a strange new territory for you and all of a sudden you're rushing in full speed ahead."

"Well, you always say I've got to take some risks. What am I supposed to do?"

"If this relationship really means something to you, why not protect it? Why not treat it as carefully as possible and give it every chance of surviving?"

"How could I do that?"

"Let me try a different approach for a moment. Let me ask you a question. What does she see in you that she likes?"

"Well, she says she likes how I look and how everyone at work thinks I'm pretty smart. But what means the most to her is that I'm thoughtful of others and gentle. She says I show others a lot of respect when I'm working with them."

"You certainly seem that way to me, too, but what do you think?"

"Oh, I don't know. You know it's hard for me to deal with all that stuff. But what's all this got to do with Debbie and me?"

"Debbie sees all sorts of things that make you lovable. So do I. If you can only begin to see and trust what Debbie and I see, then you can begin to claim your own gifts. Otherwise you'll put so much of the work on Debbie that the relationship won't have a chance."

Losers play the role of victims, and until they begin believing in themselves, their only hope is to be swept off their feet by someone else. They tend to give other people all the power: if others reject them, they're hopeless; if others love them, they're lovable. Either way—rejected or loved—Losers remain passive.

Losers work their way out of loneliness, not by adopting the Romancer's fantasy of being swept off their feet by the perfect someone, but by doing for themselves what they need to do. They make themselves more autonomous. They need to say "I can do that" instead of "I can't do anything that matters" (their typical response) or "Someone else will do it all for me" (the opposite extreme). Losers have to do their own work, but they can't do it in isolation. They need to value the affirmation they receive and build on it. Slowly but surely they will become more self-confident and, in turn, their greater self-confidence will allow them to draw closer to people and receive even more affirmation.

From Loner to Pleaser

Loners say, "I'll let you know me when I've first straightened out the mess that's inside." They may be talented and attractive and they may even know that they're talented and attractive, but they hold themselves in check. There's always something inside that needs attention before they're willing to trust themselves to others. They fear what people will say if they don't have it all "together."

Everyone is vain to some extent, but Loners don't appear to be that way at all. While most of us wouldn't pass a mirror without at least sneaking a glance, Loners could well pass right on by. But what they don't do externally, they certainly do internally. Despite their casual and seemingly unstudied appearance, they constantly check their internal mirror, constantly concerned about people's approval. They're always asking themselves, "How do I look? How do others see me?" What Pleasers are on the outside, Loners are on the inside. Loners are closeted Pleasers.

Loners are cautious in all they do, although they're less so in their work than in their relationships. As they struggle to take risks and become more active, they naturally invest more of themselves in their work. Doing things for others is a safe way for Loners to let themselves be known, and it gives them the approval they seek. The more they invest in their work, the more others praise them and the more they avoid any deeper personal commitment.

The Lone Ranger is the classic Loner. (Even his name gives him away.) Impeccably dressed, he rode into town just long enough to right a wrong, to protect a helpless person, and to battle a villain. He was marvelously adept at everything he did, but by the end of his adventure he galloped off into the sunset and someone was left behind to ask, "Who was that masked man?"

Unlike Pleasers, Loners have to become more active but, like Pleasers, they have to care less about what other people think of them. Instead of working to achieve recognition and approval, they need to seek more actively to let themselves be known and loved.

From Loneliness to Love

Learning how to love is a lot like learning how to play the piano. Beginners start by mastering a single octave, the first eight notes and the corresponding finger positions. And then they branch out, gradually learning the nearby octaves and adding chords to their repertoire. It takes practice and discipline and the willingness to strike wrong notes along the way. Often people stop before they learn the entire keyboard, and they limit what they can play and how well they can play it.

It's the same way with love. Loving doesn't come naturally. It isn't something we fall into. It's hard work and it demands practice and discipline and the willingness to make mistakes. Often we settle for learning only a small bit of what we need to know, a restricted range of relating. And our loving becomes as predictable and constrained as a beginner's playing of the piano.

We make ourselves lonely by limiting our range of relating. We restrict how we let ourselves be known and how we ask for care and share it with others. We play the same tired theme in the same tried and tested way, using the same few notes. Learning a new octave and ignoring the one we've already mastered is a step in the right direction, but we've still limited ourselves. When we learn how to play all the octaves, we increase the variety and possibilities of what might happen. The most authentic love, like the best music, draws from a whole range and a wide variety of options.

In what follows, I'll examine the strengths of each pattern—the octave they play best—and show how they can blend to form a richer more expansive repertoire of love.

Romancers have passion. They're active and alive, taking risks and making uncalculated leaps into the unknown. They're clear about what they want—love—and they invest their considerable energy into pursuing it.

Romancers invest everything into finding the one person who will truly love them. They remind us that we all need depth in our relationships, a depth that's possible only in a limited number of them. Staying on the surface isn't satisfying in the long run. We need a small inner core of people who are very special in our lives. We need one person, possibly more, to cherish us like no one else. Romancers can teach us to set priorities and choose the people we're going to love. To say "yes" to a few people, it's necessary to say "no" to others.

Pleasers are active people; they put themselves into their work. They're assertive and energetic, outgoing, friendly, and involved with a lot of people. They think about others and worry about their welfare. They're not egocentric. They're positive and optimistic, and they expect the best of themselves and others.

The Pleasers' concern for many people counterbalances the Romancers' focus on one other person. The "many" and the "one" are essential partners, and an over-reliance on either is equally unsatisfying. I picture this partnership as a series of concentric circles. As much as we need a small inner core of intimate relationships, we also need others who are supportive and accepting, some of whom are closer than others. Pleasers show us that reaching out to a number of other people provides a broader network of relationships which can complement and support the equally necessary intimate relationships.

Losers acknowledge their own faults, and they can be honest, sometimes brutally so. They tend to depend on others for their sense of self-worth. In their relationships, they feel more inclined to receive than to give, since they usually underestimate what they can contribute to others. Losers remind us that dependence and receptivity are essential ingredients of love since love is a gift and it can't be made to happen. There are parts of us that are flawed and imperfect and we all want in some way to be taken care of. Losers help us to cherish our weaknesses, to ask for love, and to make room in ourselves for others.

Loners are self-reliant, introspective, content to be by themselves, and patient. They listen well and they're nonjudgmental. Their stability comes from an inner core of strength. They work hard and quietly, without fanfare or the incessant need for approval. They don't project their problems onto others.

Loners depend on themselves and their own efforts. They have the strength we all need to develop—the strength to believe we can enter into intimate relationships without being obliterated. Their independence counterbalances the dependence of Losers. Dependence without the ability to stand alone breeds a needy sort of powerlessness, while independence without the ability to depend on others insures isolation. Both are necessary.

The one and the many, dependence and independence—these are the notes which when played together and in harmony move us from loneliness to love.

Does Love last Forever?

"To say 'I love you' is to say 'You shall never die.' "
Gabriel Marcel

"We've been pals for fourteen years. Fourteen years, can you believe it? We met in the seventh grade and we stayed friends all through high school. We even went to the same college. He was my best man when I got married and I was his when he got married. We just took each other for granted. I don't mean that in a bad sense, as if we stopped caring about each other. More the way you take your mother for granted—she's always there when you need her. I knew without thinking about it that Bill was there to talk to or go camping with or help paint the house. I never had a brother, but Bill's what I always thought a brother must be like.

"I helped him and Marge pack and I watched as the movers loaded the van. We joked about how I'd have a free place to stay whenever business takes me to New York.

"We've already planned our vacation together, but that won't be till next summer. We call each other every so often, but it's not the same thing. It's not like having him ten minutes away.

"Now there's this big hole in my life. I miss Bill and I don't want to keep on feeling like this. But I don't want to forget him or stop being friends either. I've seen that happen to too many friends when they move away from each other."

"Whatever happened to 'they lived happily ever after'?
"When Ted and I got married, we were the classic couple, supposedly made for each other. We weren't two starry-

eyed kids, either. He was twenty-eight and I was twenty-five, and we saw a counselor beforehand and everything.

"Now I'm thirty-nine and he's gone. He remarried two months after the divorce was final and moved to Michigan. I'm left with two kids, a house I can't make the payments on, and a job that barely pays for child care and food. I'll survive, I suppose, but I'm sure not in the market for another husband. Not for a while at least.

"He's the one who walked out, but I can't say I blame him. He was just the first to admit something had already died in our marriage. I didn't think love was supposed to die, not if it was the real thing. I'm still mad at him and mad at myself for letting this sort of thing happen to us. But mostly I just hurt."

"When Ginny's mother died, she and I and the kids went back for the funeral. I helped with most of the arrangements, glad I could do something to be of help.

"It's been awful ever since. I come in every so often and find Ginny crying while she's stirring something on the stove, and I can only imagine what it's like to lose your mother. My mom's still alive and it sure has made me more aware of the fact that she's not going to be around forever. But I'm still haunted by memories of the funeral and of my father-in-law at the graveside. They'd been married for fifty-two years. He just kept staring at the coffin. No tears or anything. But when the service was over and it came time to go back to the hearse, he wouldn't budge. He just sat there in one of those metal fold-up chairs under that awning they put up and stared at the coffin. Ginny's brother and I almost had to lift him by the elbows and carry him away, and you could feel something give in him. It was like a trap-door opened and his spirit dropped out. His life's just so empty now.

"I feel awful for him. And you know what's the worst of it? I find myself looking at Ginny and realizing that someday she too will die. Imagine loving someone that much and having it all taken away."

Love isn't always warm feelings and good times. Even under the best of circumstances, it's hard work, requiring an enormous amount of time and energy. We constantly put ourselves at risk. We're delighted when people love us, but we're also haunted by questions. How much should I say? How honest should I be? Am I getting too involved? Is this person worth it or am I just fooling myself? Am I setting myself up to be hurt all over again?

Love causes us so much fear and apprehension in the first place and so much pain later on. People move away, marriages end in divorce, and those who are closest to us die. Why take the risk of loving when we know that it will end?

Is there any way to keep love alive?

Love isn't a thing, a separate entity with a life all its own. It isn't something we fall into or something that comes over us like a cloud. It's a decision and—for the most part— a mutual one. It begins when we decide to love; it continues when we choose to keep investing in it; and it ends only when we resolve to let it die

Hal had been seeing me for a little over a year and a half. He was a seminarian, studying to be a priest with a religious order. He had begun making friends with some of the men in his class, and he had established one really close friendship. This made him nervous.

"What happens when we go out on our various assignments after we're ordained? Or what happens if my friend decides not to be ordained? What happens then? There's no guarantee. I may be as lonely as before."

"You're right. Love doesn't come with a guarantee. People you love may move far away. They may even die. But that doesn't mean you have to be lonely."

"What do you mean?"

"Let's use our relationship as an example. First, take a long look at me. When you're seeing me and I'm right here, it's easy to stay in this relationship. Right?"

"Right."

"Now, close your eyes. Am I still a part of your life?"

"Of course."

"But you can't see me."

"But I know you're there. It's more than simply keeping you in sight."

"Let's go one step further. Let's imagine that you walk out of this office at the end of this appointment and you go home. Now you can't see me or hear me and I'm not in your presence. Has our relationship ended?"

"No."

"Why not?"

"Well, I keep you a part of my life."

"How do you do that?"

"I think about you a lot. I imagine how you would react to certain situations. I can almost hear you saying things to me at times."

"What's that like?"

"It's as though you're with me even when we're apart. It's as though I take you with me. It's not the same thing as seeing you or being in the same room with you, but it is like being with you in a way."

"As distance increases, it's easier to forget me. And if the time between our getting together increases, it can be even easier. It takes work to keep relationships alive, but they can survive even great distances."

"That's easy with you. But how do I do that with others if they move away?"

"The same way you do it with me. You remember them. You think about them and what they would say or do. You call them on the phone. You write letters. You pray for them. There are lots of things you can do to keep love alive."

While living close to the people we love causes its own problems and tensions, physical distance adds even more stress and complications. Separation puts a strain on even the best of relationships. Some continue over time and grow stronger in spite of the distance, while others fade and grow weak. Some die altogether, and we lose touch completely with people we once loved.

We don't have to let distance destroy love, even though the loneliness of separation can be overwhelming. Letters and telephone calls—as helpful as they are—aren't enough to foster love. We have to choose to continue loving; we have to remind ourselves over and over again of how much the people we love mean to us. It takes a lot of remembering to keep another person vitally present in our lives, and it takes a lot of effort to hold onto others with our hearts and minds when they aren't close at hand. We have to prize the relationships we have and treasure them as living things, not simply as past experiences. When we enter into love, we change our entire lives. Nothing is ever the same. I've noticed how people who take up jogging alter their lives. They change their daily schedules, they watch what they eat, and they modify their smoking and drinking habits. Love demands even more basic and far-reaching changes. It causes us to alter the way we think and act and spend our time. Everything changes and we are changed in the process. We can never be the same again because of the people we've loved. Even if they move away, they can't take from us what we've gained from them. We can hold onto them at a distance and we can remember what they've meant for us. Being separated from the people we love is radically different than having never been loved at all.

Love is a decision and we can choose to nourish loving even when we're far away from the people we cherish. It's a decision that costs—perhaps more than some people can afford or are willing to pay—and that must be renewed and acted on each day and many times through the day. Distance doesn't end love unless we choose to let it.

What happens in a divorce when one person decides to stop loving and the other doesn't?

If two people have said "yes" to each other, if they've made a commitment and strengthened its bonds over time, one person can continue to say "yes" even when the other decides to say "no." Marital separation and divorce are a different form of distance—permanent and filled with pain and hard feelings—but they are still a form of distance. Often there's good reason to respond to a "no" with a "no," and the person who initially wanted to continue the relationship may well need to let go of it. But one person's decision doesn't take away another's option. Regardless of what one spouse decides in a marriage, regardless of the finality of a divorce, the other person must still make an independent decision.

What is true for marriages is true for friendships. If one person chooses to end the friendship, the other still needs to make a decision.

It's a devastating experience when someone we love dies. The loss is overwhelming and the grief seems as though it will never end. While we may not realize it at the time, death is like distance; it doesn't have the power to put an end to love. The very pain of the loss testifies to the continued importance of the other person in our lives. If we decide, we can continue loving people who have died, remembering them and their love for us, keeping a place in our hearts for them—the place they occupied while they were alive. We can keep people alive in us.

Does love end? Yes. Must love end? No. Distance, divorce, and death are occasions when love sometimes ends, but they are not the cause of its demise. Love can only end if we decide to stop loving. No one can take love from us unless we are willing to give it up. Even if someone moves away geographically or is separated by divorce or dies, we can choose—if we want to—to go on loving. Love is decision from its beginning to its end. It gives birth to great joy and great pain, and it entails risk. It isn't something that anyone can just take from us—unless we decide to let it go. Love comes to an end, then, only when we decide to let it. We can choose to stop loving, and we can choose to continue loving even in face of distance, divorce, and death. It's a decision that keeps love alive, and if you believe in a life that doesn't end—as I do—then the love we choose to give is a love that lasts forever.